W9-DFV-848

BE
TRANSFORMED

"With the gentleness gained from years of ministering to the needs and wounds of others, Bob Schuchts introduces you to the healing power of the sacraments in a powerfully eye-opening way. *Be Transformed* explains how the graces from all seven sacraments impact your daily life and how they can heal deep wounds of rejection, confusion, and abandonment. In doing so, you come to understand your true identity in Christ. After reading this book, you will realize that your deepest longings are themselves a longing for the sacraments."

Christopher West
Founder and president of *The Cor Project*
Cofounder of the Theology of the Body Institute

"For many people, the sacraments stand at a distance as a formality to the Christian life. Not fully understanding the ministry of Christ, the apostles, and the Church over the past two thousand years, many are unaware of what and who the sacraments really are and the powerful role they play in the life God designed for each of us. In this book, Bob Schuchts has recaptured the meaning and beauty of the sacraments and the powerful work of Christ through them. *Be Transformed* is a book that will stand the test of time and truly transform people's lives. This book has renewed my faith in Christ and the Church and instilled in me a new vigor for the sacraments, and I'm certain it will for you!"

Paul George
Founder of Adore Ministries

"This book helped me understand sacramental life in the Church in new ways with every passing chapter. Over the years, I have been profoundly impacted and led into healing by Bob Schuchts and his ministry—this book is, naturally, a continuation of that. As a convert to the Catholic faith who struggles with scrupulosity, my eyes are still opening to the goodness and abundant grace of the sacraments. Schuchts is intersecting sacramental theology, which can sometimes be approached hyper-academically, with the dedication to the inner healing work of the Spirit. This book has been a gift to my life!"

Audrey Assad
Catholic singer, songwriter, and musician

"What a beautifully simple and transforming book! Sadly, many Catholics don't understand and, more importantly, don't experience the full grace and power contained in the sacraments. God desires to transform, heal, and make holy his people, and he so often chooses to bring this about in the sacraments of the Church. With each sacrament, Bob Schuchts marvelously reveals the often-unseen healing grace contained within the sacraments. He goes on to show that this grace is present for all people who open their hearts to receive it."

Rev. Dave Pivonka, T.O.R.
Author of *Breath of God*

"*Be Transformed* offers a fresh and original way of understanding the ancient Catholic tradition that the sacraments heal the wounds of fallen human nature. In a world where so many have experienced deep hurts, this book is exactly what is needed! Through personal testimonies and clear explanations, Schuchts shows how every one of the sacraments can be the means of a personal encounter with the Lord Jesus, the physician of our souls and bodies."

Mary Healy
Author of *Men and Women Are from Eden*

"Bob Schuchts has masterfully illumined the healing and restorative power of the sacraments—these transforming rivers of grace that bring us into the abundant life. For lifelong Catholics or anyone who has ever wondered, 'Does anything really happen to me when I receive the sacraments?' this book is for you!"

Sr. Miriam James Heidland, S.O.L.T.
Catholic speaker and author of *Loved as I Am*

BE
TRANSFORMED

The Healing Power of the Sacraments

BOB SCHUCHTS

Ave Maria Press AVE Notre Dame, Indiana

Nihil Obstat: Héctor R.G. Pérez, S.T.D.
            Censor Librorum

Imprimatur: + Gregory L. Parkes, D.D., J.C.L.
            Bishop of Pensacola–Tallahassee

Scripture texts in this work are taken from the *New American Bible, revised edition* © 2010, 1991, 1986, 1970 Confraternity of Christian Doctrine, Washington, DC, and are used by permission of the copyright owner. All Rights Reserved. No part of the *New American Bible* may be reproduced in any form without permission in writing from the copyright owner.

© 2017 by Bob Schuchts

All rights reserved. No part of this book may be used or reproduced in any manner whatsoever, except in the case of reprints in the context of reviews, without written permission from Ave Maria Press®, Inc., P.O. Box 428, Notre Dame, IN 46556, 1-800-282-1865.

Founded in 1865, Ave Maria Press is a ministry of the United States Province of Holy Cross.

www.avemariapress.com

Paperback: ISBN-13 978-1-59471-681-2

E-book: ISBN-13 978-1-59471-682-9

Cover image © Peter Zelei/iStock.

Cover and text design by Andy Wagoner.

Printed and bound in the United States of America.

Library of Congress Cataloging-in-Publication Data is available.

DEDICATED TO ST. JOHN PAUL II

Thank you for revealing the Father's love to the whole world.
Your integral vision of the human person is the inspiration
behind this book.

We are not the sum of our weaknesses and failures; we are the sum of the Father's love for us and our real capacity to become the image of his Son.

Pope John Paul II
World Youth Day Toronto, 2002

CONTENTS

PREFACE

Soon after I published my first book, *Be Healed* (Ave Maria Press, 2014), I began to receive communications from people all over North America and beyond, telling me about their powerful encounters with Jesus through the sacraments. I heard statements such as:

- "After reading your book, I had the most powerful and life-changing confession of my life."

- "I am finally becoming the priest I always wanted to be."

- "I now see what God intended my marriage to be and why healing is so necessary for that to happen. I wish I knew this before I was married."

Others have shared about their transforming encounters with Jesus in the sacraments of Holy Communion, the Anointing of the Sick, Baptism, and Confirmation. Still others shared their excitement in gaining a whole new perspective on the sacraments. These testimonies underscored for me the hunger that many people have to understand and rediscover the life-changing power of the sacraments.

It is for this reason that I felt called to write this current book: *Be Transformed: The Healing Power of the Sacraments.* I want everyone to experience the "riches of his glory" (Eph 3:16) that are mysteriously, yet powerfully, communicated through the sacraments. Building on many of the central themes of *Be Healed*, this book underscores the often unrealized and unappreciated capacity of the sacraments to transform every area of our lives, reaching even the deepest wounds of our existence. I have come to understand that the sacraments are God's primary remedy for healing the whole person, the whole family, the whole Church, and the whole world. They are powerful because the Holy Spirit is always working in and through these sacred mysteries to usher us more fully into the resurrection life of Jesus.

I introduced many of these ideas in *Be Healed*, highlighting the vital importance of discovering our true identity as the Father's beloved, how sin and wounds distort this identity, and how the Holy Spirit working through the sacraments restores us to wholeness in Christ. This book builds on many of those themes yet stands alone. You do not need to have read *Be Healed* in order to understand and benefit from this book. Both books are meant for every reader at every stage of his or her spiritual journey.

I believe as you work your way through this book with an open heart you will discover a much greater appreciation of the sacraments. Even more importantly, my prayer is that you will *be transformed* through their healing power in ways that will deeply impact your life and all your relationships, both now and for all eternity.

INTRODUCTION

*"Do not conform yourselves to this age but
be transformed . . ."*
Romans 12:2

Transformation is an essential part of our lives as Christians. To grow spiritually, each one of us must undergo a radical process of dying and rising. Shedding the deceptive lies that keep us bound in sin and shame, we are called to embrace our true identity and unique mission in Christ. This journey is radical because it reaches the deepest roots of our brokenness, moving us out of the dark prison of our self-centeredness and into the glorious freedom of communion with the Blessed Trinity.

Over the years, as a therapist, teacher, and ministry leader, I have often reflected on the nature of this spiritual journey and how transformation is accomplished in each of our lives. Drawing on the wisdom of scripture and Church teaching, I have come to realize that the sacraments play a much more vital role in this process than I ever imagined. As a lifelong Catholic, I have not always appreciated the sacraments or comprehended how inherently powerful they are. It took me many years to understand what the Church has known and taught from the beginning: when received in faith, the sacraments have tremendous power through the Holy Spirit to radically transform our lives. The *Catechism of the Catholic Church* says, "Celebrated worthily in faith, the sacraments confer the grace that they signify. They are efficacious because in them *Christ himself is at work*: it is he who baptizes, he who acts in his sacraments in order to communicate the grace that each sacrament signifies. . . . As fire transforms into itself everything it touches, so *the Holy Spirit transforms into the divine life whatever is subjected to his power*" (*CCC*, 1127, emphasis added).

Did you catch all that? Each sacrament is a life-changing encounter with Jesus, communicated through the power of the Holy Spirit. This power dwelling within us is the very same power that raised Jesus from the dead (see Rom 8:11), communicating his supernatural life into us. Isn't that amazing? As we will see in the coming pages, the Holy Spirit working through the sacraments is literally capable of raising people from the dead—physically and spiritually. This is our call as Christians—to live Christ's resurrection life. This is why he gave us the sacraments: "The desire and work of the Spirit in the heart of the Church is that we may live the life of the risen Christ" (*CCC*, 1099).

Most of us, including myself, are still largely asleep to these realities. Though we have received the most potent force in the universe, we go around on a daily basis as if we are on our own and have to figure life out for ourselves. How can this possibly be? Why do we have this gap between what the Church teaches and our own unspectacular personal experiences with the sacraments?

The scriptures and the *Catechism* provide some much-needed insight into these matters (see *CCC*, 1098; Heb 3:12–13). They point to the condition of our *hearts* as the key factor in our yielding to the power of the Spirit in our lives. When our hearts become hardened through the deceit of sin, we inhibit the power of the Spirit working in and through us. Furthermore, when we fail to forgive those who hurt us, we create barriers which impede the flow of God's grace in our hearts (see Lk 6:37–38; *CCC*, 2840; 2843).

Conversely, when we humble ourselves and trustingly bring our brokenness to Jesus, his grace becomes most powerful in the midst of our weaknesses (see 2 Cor 12:9). Under these circumstances the sacraments are capable of healing the deepest roots of our brokenness, delivering us from the wounds of sin and bringing us back into intimate communion with the Trinity. This is what it means to *Be Transformed*.

—⟋⟍—

The sacraments are God's chosen remedy for healing our deadly wounds and infusing our souls with Christ's resurrection life. These wounds, which originated with the sin of Adam and Eve and are perpetuated and deepened by our own personal sins, keep us doubting God's love and inhibit its expression in our lives.

The Holy Spirit is always working, in and through the sacraments, to reproduce Christ's life within us. His supernatural presence expressed in every sacrament has the capacity to heal our brokenness, restore our identity, and empower us to share in Christ's relentless mission. This three-fold process of transformation—Healing, Identity, and Mission—is summarized by the acronym HIM.[1]

Healing is a life-changing encounter with God's love and truth. Whereas sin fragments us, the Father's love restores us to wholeness in Christ. This occurs most effectively through the sacraments as God's healing love reaches the depths of our being. In the words of St. John Paul II: "The Holy Spirit [working through the sacraments] . . . purifies from everything that disfigures man . . . , he heals even the deepest wounds of human existence."[2] Over time, God's healing progressively restores us to our true identity.

Identity refers to who we are and how we come to understand ourselves in relation to God. When we live apart from God and separate ourselves from his love and truth, we develop a false identity based on lies and deceptions. We end up being defined by our sins, wounds, and disordered relationships. Conversely, as we enter into a real and vibrant relationship with Jesus through the sacraments, we come to discover the truth about ourselves. St. John Paul II was fond of quoting the Second Vatican Council in this regard: "Christ, the new Adam, in the very mystery of the revelation of the Father and of his love, fully reveals man to himself and brings to light his most high calling."[3] This most high calling represents our mission.

Mission concerns our unique purpose in life, stretching us beyond our human limitations to become the unrepeatable person God created us to be. Another of St. John Paul II's favorite passages from the Second Vatican Council speaks to this reality: "Man cannot fully find himself except through a sincere gift of himself."[4] Flowing from our unique identity in Christ, our mission is tailored to fit our specific vocations and life circumstances. It informs how we invest our time, energy, and resources. Prior to surrendering our lives to God, many of us have engaged in various "pseudo-missions" which failed to call us beyond ourselves. But when inspired and empowered by the Holy Spirit, our personal mission becomes a dynamic participation in Jesus' work of restoring all things to the Father (see *CCC*, 850). When offered to God, nothing in our life is ever wasted. Even our wounds, when healed (like Christ's), become a powerful means of grace to help restore others to wholeness and holiness. Everything in our life, even our deepest brokenness, can be transformed for his glory.

In this entire process of transformation in HIM, the sacraments play the most foundational role. They are the source of our healing and restoration, they define our identity in Christ, and they empower and direct our mission. When received and lived authentically, these sacred covenants, sealed by the Lord himself, enable us to become whole and holy people (healing), knowing who we are in Christ (identity), and loving with the Father's love (mission). In this way, they bring healing not only to ourselves but also to our families and communities.

Can you imagine the impact in all of our lives if we allowed the Holy Spirit to transform us in this way through the sacraments? In the following pages you will read several heartwarming and inspiring stories of people from various vocations and states of life, whose lives and relationships have been transformed in this way. These stories of priests, married couples, single people, and consecrated religious illustrate how each of the seven sacraments has the power to heal our wounds, restore our identity, and invite us to share in Christ's mission.

—⟍⟋—

The stories, along with the practical applications throughout the book, are designed to lead you in your own process of transformation. What you are about to read has the potential to impact every aspect of your life. The first two chapters of the book provide an important context for the journey. They are intended to prepare your heart and mind for life-changing encounters with Jesus and a greater understanding of the healing power of the sacraments. Each of the remaining seven chapters (chapters 3 to 9) focuses on one of the seven sacraments, highlighting the core wounds that are healed, the identities that are bestowed, and the mission that is called forth in each sacrament. The final chapter is a conclusion, summarizing and applying the subsequent chapters in light of the movie *The Lion King*. A comprehensive prayer experience at the end of the book brings all the elements together.

Because every sacrament is for the benefit of every person, I encourage you to read the chapters in order. The graces and applications will build upon one another. For that reason, every chapter is meant for every reader. You won't need to skip the chapter focusing on Holy Orders, for example, because you aren't ordained or the one on Matrimony because you are not married. All the chapters are written for your personal benefit.

You will notice as you read through the book that God's Word and prayer are intimately tied to the sacraments and add to their efficacy in our lives. With that in mind, I have woven reflection questions, scriptural meditation, and prayer activities into every chapter to help you prayerfully contemplate the insights you receive while reading.

As you work your way through the book, I encourage you to read a chapter at a time, stopping to engage the reflection questions, immerse yourself in the selected scripture passage, and enter into greater intimacy with the Lord through prayer. Furthermore, I recommend that you form a small, trusted community to walk through this material together.

May the Holy Spirit grant you revelation and healing as you make your way through the book. May you discover more deeply your true identity in Christ. And may our eternal Father be glorified in you as his mission is more fully realized in your life.

1

UNVEILED FACES
How We Reflect God's Glory

All of us, gazing with unveiled face on the
glory of the Lord, are being transformed into
the same image from glory to glory. . . .
2 Corinthians 3:18

Pope Francis refers to Jesus as the "face of the Father's mercy."[1] I love this description because it captures the essence of Jesus' character as well as the heart of his mission. The gospels are filled with eyewitness accounts of his encounters with all kinds of broken people, including many who are sick, oppressed, or bound by the shackles of sin and shame. These accounts cover a wide range of experiences, such as the woman caught in adultery (see Jn 8:1–11); Zacchaeus, the self-serving tax collector (see Lk 19:1–10); and the little boy with the mute spirit (see Mk 9:14–29). In these stories we see Jesus' compassionate heart overflowing with the Father's merciful love.

You may have noticed that Jesus' mercy is expressed very differently in these stories depending on the way people approach him and the condition of their hearts. Not everyone in the gospel narratives seems to draw out Jesus' compassion. Even in the same gospel accounts, he interacts differently with different people. Notice, for example, his reaction to the scribes and Pharisees, who were all too eager to throw stones at the woman caught in adultery. In their pride and pompous piety, they acted as if they had no need for a savior. They elicited a much less compassionate response from the Lord—what some might call a severe mercy.

Seeing straight through the pretenses of these revered leaders, Jesus exposed the depths of their proud hearts, unmasking their hypocrisy and bringing to light the deadness behind the veneer of their whitewashed facades (see Mt 23). Have you ever wondered, as I have, whether Jesus was acting out of character in confrontations like these? Was he still the "face of the Father's mercy"? Didn't he tell us not to judge or condemn anyone and that he himself didn't come to condemn any person but to save all of us (see Lk 6:36, Jn 12:47)?

As we come to know Jesus through the gospels, we grow in trust that his judgments are pure and motivated by a perfect balance of mercy and justice, which are completely integrated in Jesus' life. Like his Father, Jesus sees beyond our external facades and into the motives and intents of our hearts (see 1 Sm 16:7). Perhaps you've noticed that he isn't easily impressed with outward appearances such as titles and degrees, worldly accomplishments, public accolades, or prominent positions when these merely serve to mask our brokenness. Hiding anything from him who sees all things is an illusion of the deadliest kind. Just ask Adam and Eve, who thought they could hide their sin from their omniscient Creator by covering themselves with fig leaves (see Gn 3).

Ever since that first sin we all have fashioned for ourselves personally tailored fig leaves. Like the Pharisees, we're all prone to veil ourselves behind masks of pride and self-righteousness, which we use to cover our inadequacies. Fr. Jacques Philippe expresses this common human condition of ours with great insight: "It is worth reflecting on the problem of pride. We are all born with a deep wound, experienced as a lack of being. We seek to compensate by constructing a self, different from our real self. This artificial self requires large amounts of energy to maintain it; being fragile, it needs protecting. Woe to anyone who contradicts it, threatens it, questions it, or inhibits its expansion. When the Gospel says we must 'die to ourselves,' it means this artificial ego, this constructed self, must die, so that the real self, given us by God, can emerge."[2] Fr. Philippe's words touch upon our deepest insecurities, don't they? Hesitant to acknowledge our deepest wounds, we conceal our true faces. In doing so, we deceive even ourselves. We end up believing that this false self is who we really are. Expending all of our energy in maintaining it, we are threatened when anyone tries to unmask us to expose our sin or weaknesses.

We may point fingers at the Pharisees, but all of us have a natural inclination to veil our faces in one way or another, as they did. But if we are to make progress spiritually, we must be willing to come before Jesus with *unveiled faces* (see 2 Cor 3:18), bringing our wounds and our shame to him, so that he can heal us and fill us with his glory. This unveiling is the first step in facing our brokenness on the road to becoming the whole person God created us to be. As we grow in humility through the working of the Holy Spirit in our lives, we gradually come to realize that we lack certain capacities on our own, most especially when it comes to receiving and expressing God's merciful love.

In this light, it becomes a bit easier to see why Jesus so passionately confronted the Pharisees. Like many of us today, they developed personally fitted fig leaves, woven together by their knowledge of the scriptures and their religious practices. They could fool many of the people with their false front, but not Jesus. Woe to Jesus for confronting and threatening their masks. Rather than die to themselves, they eventually killed him instead.

We may be aghast at the Pharisees' response, but many of us act similarly without realizing it. We *kill* the very life of Jesus within us, hiding our sin and brokenness behind our false piety. We may even approach the sacraments in this state, with a deadness of heart, showing a form of godliness while denying the healing power of the Holy Spirit inherent in the sacraments. When we practice our faith superficially in this way, we, too, *kill* the life of Jesus within our own hearts, our families, and our church communities. Everyone then lives in the same shallowness of dead religion. Have you ever experienced this?

—⁓—

The *Catechism of the Catholic Church* reminds us that "the vocation of humanity is to show forth the image of God and to be transformed into the image of the Father's only Son" (1877). That means that, in Christ, we, too, are called to reveal the "face of the Father's mercy." I believe this is one of Jesus' fundamental purposes in giving us the sacraments. When we encounter the depths of the Father's mercy ourselves (through the sacraments) we are then able to represent his image to the world around us. But what happens when we end up looking and acting more like the Pharisees than Jesus—when we participate in the sacraments like the Pharisees approached their legalistic rituals? Hiding our sin and brokenness behind our facades, we kill the life of the Spirit by our dead works.

Pope Francis has a beautiful and gentle way of helping us to see beyond our fig leaves. He recently challenged all of us to look at ourselves in the mirror of God's Word, to see where that Pharisaical spirit may have hardened our own hearts. In a daily homily, he observed: "[The Pharisees] were strong, but on the outside. They were in a cast. Their heart was very weak; they didn't know what they believed." He went on to caution: "As it was for the Pharisees, there also exists for us the danger of considering our place as better than others for the only fact of observing the rules or customs, even if we do not love our neighbor, [even if] we are hard of heart or prideful."[3]

Can't we all relate to those telltale signs of self-righteousness in some measure? Let's face it, none of us goes around and publicly proclaims our worst sins and greatest faults for the whole world to see; we naturally want to put our best face forward with the people around us. And few of us see the goodness of our neighbor without some taint of judgment or superiority. I believe we each have at least a bit of that self-righteous Pharisee in us. We find it too easy to get defensive and justify ourselves while condemning others, forgetting that we have a Redeemer who is more than capable of justifying us by his death on the cross.

The biggest problem with the Pharisees is that they were stubbornly blind and refused to see, while most of us have some desire for the Holy Spirit to provide us at least a modicum of interior vision. But even with this genuine desire, our blind spots make it hard to see ourselves clearly. The Holy Spirit gives us vision. Sometimes he puts certain people in our lives to enable us to see ourselves through God's eyes.

—∽∿—

For me, one of these life-transforming encounters took place about twenty-five years ago when I met a joy-filled and holy man from Kenya named Simeon. The first time I met Simeon he grabbed my hand and led me across a parking lot to a private meeting space. I wanted to pull my hand away, but I didn't want to offend him. So I asked if holding hands with another man was a normal custom in his country. He answered back in his broken English, "I like to get a feel for a person." I quickly responded, "Can you feel I'm uncomfortable?" After we both laughed and broke the tension, he proceeded to read my heart and reveal some of my deepest wounds while showing me where I was not living authentically.

Simeon said to me, "Bob, God is holy; you not nearly so much. But God have mercy on you, and he love you. And God have grace; he make you become more like him." (It took me a while to realize the Holy Spirit was working through Simeon to reveal another layer of my self-righteousness and ungodly self-sufficiency.) Later, Simeon encouraged me to spend time seeing myself through Jesus' eyes. "Reading God's Word," he said, "is like seeing yourself in a mirror. That's why most people don't really study the Bible; they are afraid to see themselves."

A few months later, while serving as a spiritual leader with a community of men on a Christ Renews His Parish weekend, the Holy Spirit helped me see more of my self-righteousness through the mirror of God's Word. In preparing to give a talk on "New Life in Christ," I was drawn to the parable of the Pharisee and tax collector in the Gospel of Luke (18:9–14). Reflecting on the parable, I realized it was much better to identify with the tax collector, who was painfully aware of his unworthiness before God and deeply grieved by his sin. But that is not the one in the story with whom I identified at first.

I became troubled as I discovered that my heart resonated more with the Pharisee. I could relate all too well with his self-satisfaction: "O God, I thank you that I am not like the rest of humanity—greedy, dishonest, adulterous—or even like this tax collector. I fast twice a week, and pay tithes on my whole income" (Lk 18:11–12). The irony, if you could call it that, is that I resembled that Pharisee in many ways that I had previously considered good and holy. I also fasted twice a week and tithed regularly. What cut to my heart were the sins that the Pharisee disdained among the "rest of humanity." They hit too close to home, as I had personally judged members of my family for many of those exact sins and had made inner resolutions that I would not be like them. With insight from the Holy Spirit, I finally realized that I was looking down on them for not measuring up to my standard of righteousness.

As the Spirit led me to other similar passages of scripture, he invited me to look squarely at this sin of all sins: my self-righteousness. Through these verses, it was as though Jesus delivered a one-two punch of truth to knock me off my pedestal. The first blow to my ego came through Jesus' sermon on the plain in St. Luke's gospel: "Stop judging and you will not be judged. Stop condemning and you will not be condemned. Forgive and you will be forgiven. . . . For the measure with which you measure will in return be measured out to you" (Lk 6:37–38).

A similar passage from St. Paul delivered the knockout punch: "Therefore you are without excuse, every one of you who passes judgment. For by the standard by which you judge another you condemn yourself, since you, the judge, do the very same things" (Rom 2:1).

I was especially troubled by this last line: "You the judge do the very same things." How could that be? No one around me had ever accused me of being greedy, and I wasn't cheating on my taxes or having an adulterous affair. How could I be doing the same things as those I had judged? I didn't want to face the reality that I am just as much a sinner as the people who hurt me. That would mean that I am not really better than anyone else and that I, too, need a savior just like them. My false self-image couldn't bear to face that I am greedy, dishonest, and adulterous like the rest of humanity.

I had kept any semblance of those sins hidden from my self-awareness. When I did anything even remotely related to those sins, I would mercilessly condemn myself as I had condemned others. In order to be good enough in my own mind, to be loved by God, I strived to be morally perfect. Since I couldn't be perfect, I had to convince myself that I was righteous enough for God to love me, but I never knew exactly where that line was drawn. What would I do (or fail to do) that would get me on God's bad side and become one of the goats that were sent away to hell (see Mt 25:32–33)? I found myself on a hopeless and joyless treadmill, striving to be good enough but never quite measuring up. I wish I could say this is completely in my past and that I am completely free from this kind of thinking, but the truth is I still can look at God, myself, and those around me with this kind of legalistic and fearful attitude at times. Can you relate to this perfectionistic trap at all in your life? Be careful not to dismiss it too quickly. Just because you don't see it doesn't mean that you are free from it.

For me, the roots trace back to early in my life (and probably eons before that to Adam and Eve and original sin). I remember, as a child, confusing my dad's anger with God's wrath whenever I did something wrong. I wanted to please, so I did what I could to gain both of my parents' approval. When I did something wrong, I didn't want my parents or God to see my sin for fear that I would be punished and my "good boy" image would be tarnished.

I remember, as early as six years old, consciously hiding my sins from my parents. My brother Dave and I secretly smoked cigarettes on our way to school, and he made me promise I would not tell our parents. I easily agreed because I didn't want to get into trouble. At eight, I began to steal candy at a local grocery store and look at *Playboy* magazines with my friends. I lied to cover it up, which only took me deeper into hiding. Though I had the availability of the sacrament of Reconciliation, I continued to keep these sins hidden even from the priest. In sixth grade, when I became an altar boy, these patterns were well established in my life. I was already "greedy" (stealing), "dishonest" (lying), and "adulterous" (lusting after women in those magazines). I was more like the tax collector and the rest of humanity than I wanted to admit, but I kept all this hidden behind my "good boy Bob" image.

By seventh grade, when our family started unraveling due to my dad's drinking and adultery, my Pharisee suit was pretty firmly established and those tax-collector traits were kept hidden away in shame. With my heart barricaded by shame and self-righteousness, it was only natural that I would suppress my fear and pain, just as I had kept my sins hidden all those years. By ninth grade, my dad and older brother left the family, and I was primed to take on the role of family savior, hoping to avoid falling into disgrace as they had. My self-justifying attitude, now firmly entrenched, necessitated a continual drive to moral perfectionism.

—⧟—

Let me be perfectly clear. This is not the kind of perfection that Jesus calls each of us to in the Gospel. The quest for genuine holiness is not based on self-righteous striving to be good enough in order to be loved; it is the perfection of mercy, which is the true measure of holiness (see *CCC*, 1709; Lk 6:36). "It comes from an entirely free gift of God" and leads us to enter into "the divine joy" (*CCC*, 1722). Fr. Jacque Philippe notes: "Our Father in heaven does not love us because of the good that we do. He loves us for ourselves, because he has adopted us as his children forever. This is why humility, spiritual poverty is so precious."[4] True holiness is an easy yoke that comes from learning meekness and humility from Jesus (see Mt 11:29). It stands in stark contrast to the heavy yoke of legalism with which the Pharisees burdened their followers (see Mt 23:4).

God's grace is the totally unmerited gift of his love that enables us to participate in his inner life and thus discover our true identity (see *CCC*, 1995–1999). Grace can come to us in many ways. God's Word, the sacraments, and prayer are three primary ways that the Lord ordinarily communicates his graciousness to us. My friend Simeon taught me something about grace and pointed me to the scriptures as a way of seeing myself in the mirror. I want to pay his gift forward and invite you to see yourself in the mirror, too, with unveiled faces. As Simeon said, "God is good and holy; you not nearly so much. But God have mercy and God have grace."

Let's pause here a moment to reflect on what we have discussed.

Take a Moment

1. What are your thoughts after reading Fr. Philippe's insights on pride and humility? How do you hide your wounds and sins?

2. What aspects of my story and experience with Simeon relate to your life?

My friend Simeon helped me see myself through God's eyes and pointed me to scripture as a way of continuing that process. As Simeon invited me, I now invite you to hold my hand (metaphorically speaking) so that we can take a walk and look in the mirror together. Our "mirror" for this spiritual exercise comes from the Gospel of Luke, and it is the one Pope Francis chose to announce the Jubilee Year of Mercy. You are probably familiar with the story where Jesus is invited to Simon's house for dinner and they are interrupted by an unexpected guest—a sinful woman from town (see Lk 7:36–50). In some ways, this is another version of the Pharisee and the tax collector, only it is a real interaction and not a parable. As we reflect on this gospel together, remember our goal is to shed the masks of our false selves so that we can receive the abundant mercy God pours out to us and live more fully from our true identity in Christ.

As we walk through the narrative, I encourage you to take note of which of the main characters you identify with the most. First we meet the Pharisee, Simon, who is Jesus' host. An upstanding citizen and well respected in his community, he most likely practiced his faith diligently and was well regarded by his influential friends. Next we have the unnamed "sinful woman." She apparently has an unsavory reputation and was not among the invited guests. Finally we have Jesus, the guest of honor.

Here is how the story unfolds: While Jesus is interacting with Simon and his guests the woman barges into Simon's home unannounced. Oblivious to the host and the other guests, she makes a beeline to Jesus, sobbing as she wipes his feet with her tears. She then dries them with her hair, proceeds to kiss Jesus' feet, and pours a costly bottle of sweet-smelling ointment over them. You can imagine Simon's indignation as all this is taking place. Jesus, on the other hand, seems unfazed by this woman's invasion into the party. In fact, he receives her gift of tears and repentance and praises her for her generosity. Jesus seems more concerned about Simon's chagrin, so he engages him in a parable about two people who owe a large amount of money. It is here we pick up the interaction involving Jesus, Simon, and the woman, after Jesus proposes a parable to Simon about two debtors who owe different amounts.

Jesus (to Simon): "Which of [the forgiven debtors] will love him more?"

Simon (to Jesus): "The one I suppose whose larger debt was forgiven."

Jesus (to Simon): "You have *judged rightly*. . . . Do you *see* this woman? When I entered your house, you did not give me water for my feet, but she has bathed them with her tears and wiped them with her hair. You did not give me a kiss, but she has not stopped kissing my feet since the time I entered. You did not anoint my head with oil, but she anointed my feet with ointment. So I tell you her many sins are forgiven; hence she has shown great love. But the one to whom little is forgiven, loves little."

Jesus (to the woman): "Your sins are forgiven."

Guests (to each other): "Who is this who even forgives sins?"

Jesus (to the woman): "Your faith has saved you, go in peace."

—◈—

I love Pope Francis's reflections on this gospel when he introduced his intentions for the Jubilee Year of Mercy. Though a bit lengthy, it is well worth our time. By challenging us out of our comfort zones, he calls us to set aside our Pharisaical ways and to identify with the faith, hope, and love of the woman who knows she has nothing to lose because apart from Jesus she has nothing. Then at the end of his reflection, Pope Francis invites us to imitate the boundless mercy exemplified by Jesus:

> The gospel we have heard (cf. Lk 7:36–50) opens for us a path of hope and comfort. It is good that we should feel that same compassionate gaze of Jesus upon us, as when he perceived the sinful woman in the house of the Pharisee. In this passage two words return before us with great insistence: love and judgment. There is the love of the sinful woman, who humbles herself before the Lord; but first there is the merciful love of Jesus for her, which pushes her to approach. Her cry of repentance and joy washes the feet of the Master, and her hair dries them with gratitude; her kisses are pure expression of her affection; and the fragrant ointment poured out with abundance attests how precious he is to her eyes. This woman's every gesture speaks of love and expresses her desire to have an unshakeable certainty in her life: that of being forgiven. And Jesus gives this assurance: welcoming her, he demonstrates God's love for her, just for her! Love and forgiveness are simultaneous: God forgives her much, everything, because "she loved much" (Lk 7:47); and she adores Jesus because she feels that in him there is mercy and not condemnation. Thanks to Jesus, God casts her many sins away behind him, he remembers them no more (cf. Is 43:25). For her, a new season now begins; she is reborn in love, to a new life.
>
> This woman has really met the Lord. In silence, she opened her heart to him; in pain, she showed repentance for her sins; with her tears, she appealed to the goodness of God for forgiveness. For her, there

will be no judgment except that which comes from God, and this is the judgment of mercy. The protagonist of this meeting is certainly the love that goes beyond justice.

Simon the Pharisee, on the contrary, cannot find the path of love. He stands firm upon the threshold of formality. He is not capable of taking the next step to go meet Jesus, who brings him salvation. Simon limited himself to inviting Jesus to dinner, but did not really welcome him. In his thoughts, he invokes only justice, and in so doing, he errs. His judgment on the woman distances him from the truth and does not allow him even to understand who his guest is. He stopped at the surface; he was not able to look to the heart. Before Jesus' parable and the question of which servant would love his master most, the Pharisee answered correctly, "The one to whom the master forgave most." And Jesus does not fail to make him observe: "Thou hast judged rightly" (Lk 7:43). Only when the judgment of Simon is turned toward love: then is he in the right.

The call of Jesus pushes each of us never to stop at the surface of things, especially when we are dealing with a person. We are called to look beyond, to focus on the heart to see how much generosity everyone is capable. No one can be excluded from the mercy of God; everyone knows the way to access it and the Church is the house that welcomes all and refuses no one. Its doors remain wide open, so that those who are touched by grace can find the certainty of forgiveness. The greater the sin, so much the greater must be the love that the Church expresses toward those who convert.[5]

Pope Francis's insights from this gospel story are both profound and convicting. Like Simon, many of us find it difficult "to find the path of love" and to live freely from our hearts. We stop at the surface of things and don't see deeply into the hearts of the people. Our judgments distance us from Jesus, from the truth, and from the people we are judging. How often do we let formality keep us disconnected from our own hearts, as well as from Jesus? Do we love him with our whole heart like the woman did? Or do we "love" more like Simon, keeping a polite distance and welcoming Jesus into our external lives but not into our hearts?

As I read Pope Francis's comments, I couldn't help but think of how many of us approach Jesus through the scriptures, sacraments, and prayer with the same kind of formality that Simon did. Most of us lack the passionate, no-holds-barred love that the woman exhibits in seeking Jesus' love and forgiveness. Rather, we tend to find comfort in our formality and keep Jesus close enough to validate us but not so close that our self-sufficiency is threatened. We are often more concerned with maintaining our reputation and control rather than being radical, sold-out lovers of the One who gave up everything for our sake.

When Jesus gave us the sacraments of our redemption, they literally cost him everything—his entire life. He poured out his tears and his blood for us like the woman poured out her tears and ointment. He did not intend for our faith practices to be meaningless rituals of formality where we keep our polite distance. Rather, he desires for them to be living encounters with him, enabling us to die to our false selves, so that the Holy Spirit can fill us to overflowing with Jesus' resurrection life (see *CCC*, 1091–1092).

As you can readily observe from the story of Simon and the woman, it makes a huge difference how we move toward Jesus. If we approach Jesus with a false persona (external conformity without a heart conversion) we will keep a distance from him, like Simon did. We will fail to reflect his glory and remain self-satisfied in our vainglory. But if we open our hearts and face our brokenness, like the woman, we can begin to live from our true selves as we encounter his real presence in word, sacrament, and prayer. The disposition of our hearts makes all the difference.

The Church teaches that the disposition of our hearts does not limit the amount of grace Jesus gives to us as a free gift. But it does restrict how much grace we *receive* in our sacramental encounters with

Jesus. The degree of openness and belief in our hearts is the defining factor in whether the sacraments produce fruit in our lives and how much (see *CCC*, 1098). Since our hearts are the place of our encounter with Jesus, our receptivity makes all the difference (see *CCC*, 2563).

Like many of the Pharisees, we are more than capable of performing our faith practices with a proud, hardened, or disconnected heart. The *Catechism* calls this outward practice of our faith without an engagement of the heart "superstition," which is "to attribute the efficacy of prayers or sacramental signs to their mere external performance, apart from the interior dispositions they demand" (*CCC*, 2111). I wonder how many of us are practicing superstition without even realizing it.

Our heavenly Father is merciful. Wherever we are in our spiritual journey, we do not need to remain masked by pride and vainglory like Simon or veiled by our shame and disgrace like the woman before her repentance. The Father sees everything about us and accepts us as we are. But he also calls us to come out from behind our veiled faces, covered by pride and shame, so that we can receive his mercy. The more open we are to receiving all that the Father has for us the more we will be transformed into the image of Jesus. That is how we reflect his glory, by allowing ourselves to be transformed, with unveiled faces gazing on the Lord (see 2 Cor 3:18).

Let's take a moment to "look in the mirror," allowing Jesus to show us ourselves.

Take a Moment

1. In what ways are you like Simon, the woman, and Jesus? Be specific.

2. Do you see any evidence of your heart being hardened? Explain.

3. How can you tell when your faith practices are superstitious rather than genuine encounters with Jesus?

4. Describe a personal experience of an encounter with Jesus through scripture, sacrament, or prayer.

Scripture Meditation

The following passage from Luke 18 shares the story of the Pharisee and the tax collector and is classic for revealing the Pharisee in us. But more than that, it is a demonstration of God's mercy toward all of us.

I encourage you to pray with this passage as you do the following:

1. First read it for overall context.

2. Read it again, putting your name in place of references to the Pharisee.

3. Record in a journal what you see about yourself.

4. Read it one last time slowly, and replace references to the tax collector with your name. Then record what the Holy Spirit reveals to you.

Parable of the Pharisee and the Tax Collector

"[Jesus] then addressed this parable to those who were convinced of their own righteousness and despised everyone else. 'Two people went up to the Temple area to pray; one was a Pharisee and the other was a tax collector. The Pharisee took up his position and spoke this prayer to himself, "O God, I thank you that I am not like the rest of humanity—greedy, dishonest, adulterous—or even like this tax collector. I fast twice a week, and I pay tithes on my whole income." But the tax collector stood off at a distance and would not even raise his eyes to heaven but beat his breast and prayed, "O God, be merciful to me a sinner." I tell you, the latter went home justified, not the former; for everyone who exalts himself will be humbled, and the one who humbles himself will be exalted'" (Lk 18:9–14).

Let Us Pray

As we see with the tax collector and the sinful woman, God's mercy is activated when we humble ourselves in prayers of repentance. The following prayer is focused on repentance from judgments. When prayed from the heart, it enables us to renounce our self-righteousness and humble ourselves to receive God's mercy. This prayer, repeated often with specific application to areas of your judgments, will help soften your heart and break the power of pride and self-condemnation in your life.

Repentance from Judgments

Father, I acknowledge that I have judged (name of person).[6] I realize that this judgment is sin and that it keeps my heart hardened in unforgiveness and blocks the flow of your mercy and grace in my life. I am sorry for sinning against you and (name of person). Please forgive me and release me from the condemnation.

I now renounce these specific judgments (identify them one at a time). I know I cannot change my own heart, so I ask you to give me your heart of compassion and mercy for this person (name of person judged). Please bless them now, specifically in those ways exactly opposite to how I have judged them in my thoughts, words, or actions. I ask this in Jesus' name. Amen.

2

GOD'S POWERFUL BLESSINGS

How the Sacraments Restore Us to Wholeness

You are my beloved Son;
with you I am well pleased.

Luke 3:22

In the last chapter we had an opportunity to take a long look in the mirror, to really see ourselves in one of three persons representing three different aspects of ourselves: Simon the Pharisee, the sinful woman, and Jesus. These three images also represent stages of our spiritual journey. If we are honest with ourselves, we can recognize a part of ourselves in each of the people in the story.

Like the Pharisee, we, too, are prone to hide our deficiencies and weaknesses behind a facade of self-righteousness, leaving our hearts hardened and unreceptive to God's grace. Once these masks of pride are removed, we realize that we can also identify with the sinful woman. Facing our sin and wounds, we come to recognize our tremendous need for healing. Only with our faces unveiled in this way are we able to look intently at Jesus and receive his merciful love. Gazing upon him, we eventually become like him, with unveiled faces reflecting his glory (see 2 Cor 3:18, 1 Jn 3:2). This is the goal of our spiritual life: to be transformed into the image of Christ so that we share in the divine intimacy that he enjoys with the Father and the Holy Spirit.

No matter where we are in our spiritual journey, the sacraments play a key role in our transformation. If we are stuck in pride and

self-righteousness, like Simon, the sacraments of Jesus' presence con-
front us with the truth about ourselves and give us the grace to soften
our hearts. When we humble ourselves and recognize our need for
a savior, like the woman, these same sacraments effectively cleanse
us of our sin, heal the wounds and curses caused by sin, and bestow
on us the blessing of our new identity in Christ. Then, as we grow
in communion with Jesus, we become a source of his blessing to all
those around us. The more we grow in union with Jesus the more
fully we are able to enter into his mission "to make men share in the
communion between the Father and the Son in their Spirit of love"
(*CCC*, 850).

God's blessings are powerful. Yet when most of us hear the word
"blessing" we go to sleep. We too easily reduce blessing to a quick
prayer before meals or a response to someone sneezing: "God bless
you." In our ordinary vocabulary "blessing" seems rather bland and
perfunctory. But God's blessings are so much more. The *Catechism*
provides much-needed insight into this most profound reality: "God,
infinitely perfect and *blessed in himself*, in a plan of sheer goodness
freely created man to make him share in his own blessed life" (*CCC*,
1, emphasis added); "From the beginning until the end of time the
whole of God's work is a blessing" (*CCC*, 1079, emphasis added);
"Blessing is a divine and life-giving action, the source of which is
the Father; his blessing is both *word* and *gift*" (*CCC*, 1078, emphasis
added).

From these descriptions, we are able to identify three important
dimensions of blessing: (1) Blessing originates in the Father, who is
eternal blessedness; (2) Blessing is the work of God, where he communicates his life to us; and (3) Blessing is actively communicated
through both word and gift. Among all the words the Father speaks to
bless us, Jesus is the fullest expression of his word and therefore the
greatest possible blessing (see Jn 1:1). Likewise, of his many gracious

gifts, the Holy Spirit is by far his greatest gift in which all other gifts find their meaning (see Acts 2:38).

Can you see from this how the sacraments are powerful expressions of God's blessing? "Through his word, he pours into our hearts the gift that contains all gifts, the Holy Spirit" (*CCC*, 1082). Isn't this awe-inspiring? The almighty God who created the universe freely pours himself into us through these sacred mysteries. Wow! What could possibly be more incredible and powerful than this?

We gain a glimpse of the divine power of the sacraments by observing the Father's blessing of Jesus at his Baptism. This marker event in Jesus' life is the source and prototype for all the sacraments of the new covenant. Listen attentively to the Father's affirming words as he blesses the Eternal Word: "You are my beloved Son; with you I am well pleased" (Lk 3:22). These words of delight from the Father affirm Jesus' true identity as his beloved. The Father then confirms his words by pouring out the gift of his Holy Spirit, who descends upon Jesus and remains with him, anointing him with power for his messianic mission.

This action of the Father at Jesus' Baptism in many ways repeats the blessing that occurred at the moment of Jesus' conception, when the angel Gabriel proclaimed to Mary, "The Holy Spirit will come upon you, and the power of the Most High will overshadow you. Therefore the child to be born will be called holy, the Son of God" (Lk 1:35). Notice again how dynamically God's Word and Spirit work together to communicate the Father's blessing, forming Jesus into the word made flesh.

In his book *Unbound*, Neal Lozano astutely observes that Jesus' entire life is an ongoing participation in the Father's blessing. The Father blessed Jesus not once or twice but continuously. At the major turning points of his life, the Father proclaimed these blessings publicly: "Jesus received special blessings of his identity and destiny at his conception, during his time in the womb, at his birth, through his circumcision and dedication, at his baptism, and at the major points of his life, prior to going to the cross."[1]

Through each one of these outpourings of grace, the Father affirmed Jesus' identity for all to hear, while the Holy Spirit communicated the Father's love intimately. No matter how often the world *cursed* or *praised* Jesus, he did not receive his identity from their human perceptions of him. His identity remained firmly grounded in the Father's blessing. That is why Jesus never assumed a false identity from the world or from the father of lies.

And so it should be in each of our lives. God's blessing affirms us in the truth of who we are and enables us, through the Holy Spirit, to live authentically, with ever-greater confidence in God's purposes. Lozano elaborates: "As we find our identity in Jesus, we receive the very blessings that he received from the Father when he took on our humanity. Just as Mary was an instrument of that blessing to Jesus . . . so the Church, the 'body of Jesus,' is meant to be an instrument of the blessing that is ours in Christ."[2] As with Jesus, the Father continually blesses us. He offers special blessings at all the major turning points in our life: "The seven sacraments touch all the stages and all the important moments of Christian life: they give birth and increase, healing and mission to the Christian's life of faith" (*CCC*, 1210).

Jesus' Baptism provides a blueprint for the way the Father consecrates each one of us through the sacraments. We see in this hallowed event the power of God's Word, communicated in the midst of the sacrament of Baptism and received in the power of the Spirit through prayer. Every sacrament, modeled after Jesus' Baptism, is a proclamation of God's powerful word of benediction upon us, confirming our true identity and mission in Christ.

—m—

Curses are the antithesis of blessing (see Lk 6:20–26). They bring death and difficulty in place of life and goodness (see Dt 28). Curses are deceptive and destructive words and actions that tear us down, weaken our resolve, and belittle us. Though originating in the father of lies, curses usually come from the sins of others, who themselves have been infected by similar wounds and curses. These sinful words and actions can leave devastating and lasting effects upon our identity while infesting our souls with the debilitating lies of the evil one. Sowing into our souls and bodies seeds of discord and discouragement, over time the evil one's curses can cause disease and eventually death (see Jas 3:8–10, Dt 28).

When received into our spirit, these destructive words and actions have the power to form our identity in falsehood. We end up believing lies about ourselves, God, and each other. Unlike blessings, which confirm our true identity and give us life and health, these curses only serve to reinforce our false selves, stealing from us the joy and fulfillment that Jesus promised us (see Jn 10:10, 15:11).

All of us know the experience of having curses hurled against us through the verbal assaults of others. Growing up in my neighborhood, we used to shield off these curses with a familiar retort: "Sticks and stones can break my bones, but words can never hurt me." We were wrong, of course, about the power of words. Words can and often do hurt us, just as actions can, when they take hold in our being. And bones usually heal much faster than our wounded souls after they have been injured by the insults and curses of another.

The Bible makes it very clear that words and thoughts are dynamic forces that can spread good or evil. Containing spiritual power, they have the ability to bless or to curse. St. James doesn't mince any words when speaking about these realities: "No human being can tame the tongue. It is a restless evil, full of deadly poison. With it we bless the Lord and Father, and with it we curse human beings who are made in the likeness of God. From the same mouth come blessing and cursing" (Jas 3:8–10).

—⁂—

The power of human words to bless and curse took on a new depth of meaning for me several years ago while sitting at a friend's house waiting for him to come home. To pass the time, I started flipping through a large picture book on the table next to me. The more I looked and read the more interested I became, realizing that the author was giving scientific verification of the spiritual power of the spoken word. Immediately, I thought of the above scripture verses from James.

The book, *The Hidden Messages in Water,* written by Japanese scientist Masaru Emoto, turned out to be a *New York Times* best seller. He conducted his research to find out if words and thoughts have power in themselves to define reality. Speaking words of blessing and cursing into containers of water, he subsequently froze the water and photographed it. Sounds strange, doesn't it? Yet Dr. Emoto had a purpose. He wanted to find out how spoken words could impact the molecular structure in water. This could give insight to the effect words and thoughts have on our health and well-being (since our bodies are made up of 70 percent water and our brains 80 percent water).

Using a microscope, Emoto examined the molecular formations in the frozen water and then photographed each of them. The results were breathtaking and exactly what the Word of God had predicted. Words, spoken with conviction, really do have a tremendous impact to bless and to curse. Words like *happy*, *good*, and *love* produced beautiful and complex images full of light in the frozen water. Words like *depressed*, *bad*, and *hate* resulted in dark, dense, and ugly images when the molecular structures were closely examined.

After conducting a similar study with cooked rice, Emoto found the "blessed" rice remained white after thirty days of receiving the words "I love you" whereas the "cursed" rice became black and then decayed after thirty days of repeating the phrase "You fool." Emoto also tested the power of prayer, and the results were equally amazing. Prayer, a primary means of calling upon God's blessing, has an even greater power to shape and define reality.[3]

—〰—

Dr. Emoto's research confirmed what the Bible has said all along: words convey spiritual realities and are indeed quite powerful.

Hurtful words, received into our souls, can damage us for a lifetime. In the same way, words of blessing can transform our lives for good. We all know this from our own experience. But there is another crucial factor to consider in all of this. We are human beings with minds and wills, not simply passive containers of water or clumps of rice. Most of the time, we can actively choose what we believe and what we allow to impact us. In our childhood saying about sticks and stones, we discovered a partial truth after all. We do have the ability to shield against words and thoughts from harming us by choosing to resist or renounce their power. Our reception or resistance plays a huge role.

Hurtful words and other curses impact us to the degree we allow them to take up residence in our being. Author John Eldredge contends that we can ward off the damaging impact of verbal assaults by choosing not to agree with the lies of the enemy.[4] Mostly, it is up to us whether we allow words to find a home in our thoughts. With words that have already affected us, we can renounce them and overcome them by responding to a curse with a blessing (see Mt 5:44). This, I believe, is what wise Solomon meant when he said "a curse uncalled for never lands" (Prv 26:2).

This truth works both ways. Just as evil words, thoughts, and actions only hurt us when we receive them into our hearts and believe them, the same is true with blessings. We only receive the powerful effects of blessings in our lives when we let them into our spirits and give them the power to take root in our minds and hearts. Do you see why faith is so crucial in our spiritual lives, including how we approach the sacraments?

What do you believe about the power of words, thoughts, and prayers to bless and to curse? Let's take a moment to explore this further.

Take a Moment

1. What is your reaction to Emoto's research on the power of words and thoughts?

2. What role do you think faith and agreements play in the way we receive blessings and curses?

3. Identify two specific ways you have been blessed and cursed. How did these influence the way you see yourself (your identity)?

After pondering the connection between Dr. Emoto's research and St. James's exhortation, I felt prompted to study other scripture passages and to see what the Church teaches about blessing. What I discovered continues to inspire me, and it also has given me greater insight into the healing power of the sacraments. I began to realize that the sacraments, invoked by God's powerful words and infused by the Holy Spirit, mark the beginning of the "new creation" (2 Cor 5:17). As such, they follow the same pattern as the first creation, when God called all things into being through his unfailing word and Spirit (see Gn 1).

Have you ever noticed this phenomenon throughout the Bible? When the Almighty speaks, amazing things happen, sometimes gradually and at other times instantly. God's word is powerful and effective, always creating and shaping reality wherever it is spoken (see Is 55:11, Heb 4:12). We see this pattern beginning in the book of Genesis, when God *commanded creation into existence.* "From the very beginning God blessed all living beings, especially man and woman" (*CCC*, 1080).

Meditating on the creation story, I noted that when God created the world through his words and Spirit, everything was created to be a gift for us. He then blessed every single part and particle of his creation! He spoke into the water (and probably the rice, too) and called it "good." (As it turns out, Emoto was merely imitating God.) When God created human beings, however, he gave us a double blessing, infusing our soul with his own Spirit and proclaiming that we are "very good" (Gn 1:26–31).

Let me say that again (because we need to let it penetrate our hearts). God himself blessed you and me from the very beginning. He called us *very good* because we are made in his image and likeness, and he breathed his Spirit into us. His divine nature lives in us. Why do we have such a difficult time believing all this? Is it because we have allowed the curses resulting from our wounds and sins to define our identity? This is the conclusion I came to as I continued to study the scriptures.

We know from the Bible and Church teaching that the entire human race lost the blessing of paradise when our first parents allowed themselves to be deceived by the father of lies and rejected the Father's blessing (see Gn 3:1–15, Jn 8:41–45). This is why St. John Paul II concludes, "At the root of human sin is the lie which is a radical rejection of the truth contained in the word of the Father."[5] Under Satan's influence, Adam and Eve denied not only the goodness of God but also their own goodness. By their free choice, they invited Satan's diabolical curses into the world and into their own bodies and souls by believing his lies about the Father and themselves. They ruined paradise (a state of perpetual blessing) not only for themselves but also for all the rest of God's creation.

In Adam and Eve's denial of God's goodness, they turned their backs on his never-failing love and generosity, thereby losing the precious gifts of communion, security, and eternal life for all of us (see Gn 2 and 3). Though God still loved and protected them, our first parents became afraid and hid in shame. They could no longer believe in God's love or feel his presence. They most likely felt helpless, hopeless, and confused. Thus the seven deadly wounds were introduced into human consciousness. Since that time our personal sins continue to perpetuate these deadly wounds and keep us bound in identity lies.

Wounds	Identity Lies
Rejection	I am not loved; I am not wanted.
Abandonment	I am alone; no one cares.
Powerlessness	I feel overwhelmed; I can't do anything.
Confusion	I don't understand; it doesn't make sense.
Fear	If I trust I will be hurt; I'm not safe.
Shame	I am bad, dirty, stupid, etc.; it's all my fault.
Hopelessness	Things will never change; I'm weary.

—⟪⟫—

Notice in the table above how each of the seven deadly wounds is accompanied by corresponding identity lies. These lies powerfully impact what we believe about ourselves and effectively block our ability to receive the Father's blessings in our life. For example, if you carry around a wound of rejection you may believe that you are not loved or wanted, even by God. You may live in self-rejection and without knowing it reject the love coming from the people around you. In such a scenario, it may be quite difficult to accept your true and eternal identity as the Father's beloved. This same pattern holds with each of the deadly wounds. Identity lies keep us from knowing our true identity and living in the fullness God has for us. Remember St. John Paul II's insight: at the root of sin is the *lie*, which rejects the Father's goodness.

Do you see from this why *sin* is such a terrible reality? By blocking the Father's blessing, sin separates us from life in the Spirit and infects the whole human race with the lies of the evil one. The wounds of sin effectively cut us off from the Father's love and destroy and hinder the flow of goodness and blessing that the Father desires to pour out upon his children out of his sheer graciousness (see Jas 1:14–17). To add insult to injury, after the father of lies turns us away from God, he then convinces us that our defects make us unlovable.

Each area of wounding then becomes the fertile soil for the enemy's lies to be implanted in our minds and hearts. Over time, these wounds and lies from the evil one become the foundation for our false identity. Weakening our resolve and belittling our dignity, they disfigure the image of God within us. These deeply rooted identity lies distort the vision we have of ourselves. They also distort our perceptions of others, leading us to judge them falsely. Most importantly, they skew our perceptions of God, preventing us from seeing his goodness and from trusting him with our whole heart. These lies can remain influential in our lives long after they gain access through the wounding effects of sin. Even after we have received the gift of the Spirit through the sacraments, these wounds and lies can still keep us imprisoned in a false identity.

As I have journeyed with many people in their healing process over the years, I have come to see that all of us have been affected by these lies about ourselves and God. In one way or another, we have each been plagued by all seven of these deadly wounds. As I mentioned earlier, I believe they are the primordial effects of original sin.[6] We may not immediately recognize these wounds and lies in our lives because many of us have hidden our brokenness, even from ourselves. But underneath these facades, we are all wounded in similar ways.

Though the circumstances of our wounding differ greatly in magnitude, these wounds have been passed down from generation to generation, through our personal sins and the sins of others. No one is exempt. These deadly wounds (rejection, abandonment, shame, fear, confusion, powerlessness, and hopelessness) are universal.[7] They are both cause and consequence of our personal sin.[8]

—m—

Isn't it clear from everything we have been discussing that we desperately need a redeemer, one willing to take on all of these curses on the cross and return only blessings in their place (see Gal 3:13, Lk 6:28)? This is the primary reason Jesus came to earth—to reveal to us the true image of the Father and to restore in creation all that has been wounded by the curse of sin. Everywhere he went, his words and actions became signs of the Father's presence and blessing (see Jn 2:11). Jesus knew his true identity and lived in constant communion with the Father.

Through Jesus' powerful spoken words and gestures, blessings transformed curses, and simple matter became infused with supernatural grace. Blind eyes regained sight (see Mk 8:22–25); sinners received forgiveness (see Lk 5:20); water turned into wine (see Jn 2:1–11); and after Jesus' powerful words of blessing, blessed bread miraculously became his body and wine was changed into his blood (see Mt 26:26–28). Through his words, spoken in the authority of his Father and empowered by the Holy Spirit, Jesus literally redefined reality and redeemed creation. He went beyond just overturning the curses from the fall; he converted these curses into even greater blessings. His crucifixion and resurrection are the most astounding examples of how blessings triumph over curses.

Faith, of course, played a vital role in all Jesus accomplished, just as it does in our lives. Believing his Father would do what he promised, Jesus spoke with complete authority and trust in his Father's powerful words (see Mk 1:22). Sadly, most of the people with whom Jesus interacted did not believe his words and misinterpreted his actions. They suffered as a result of their unbelief; they did not receive the abundant blessings that Jesus longed to give them (see Mt 13:58, Jn 6:66). In stark contrast, those who did believe Jesus' teachings and sought his healing touch became increasingly more whole as they graciously basked in his divine blessing (see Mt 12:15, Lk 6:19). The Beatitudes show us that to receive God's blessing, we must come with humility and childlike faith: "Blessed are the poor in Spirit, for theirs is the kingdom of heaven" (Mt 5:3).

Jesus formed his disciples to trust in the Father's goodness with child-like faith. Eventually, he entrusted them with the same authority and power to bless that he received from his Father. They in turn passed on this same power and authority to others who were poor in spirit so that the Father's mission of transformation would continue until Jesus returned (see Acts 20:28; *CCC*, 861). This passing on of the Father's authority to bless is the origin and purpose of Holy Orders and the fountainhead for all the other sacraments.

In the holy sacraments he instituted, Jesus himself is alive and present, acting through his word and pouring out his Spirit. He continues to carry out his work of blessing through his chosen representatives. As Fr. Dave Pivonka, T.O.R., affirms in his book *Breath of God,* Jesus continues this supernatural work through the simple elements of nature: "What a tremendous gift we have in the sacraments, the channels of grace the Lord has chosen to use for our sanctification and salvation! Every time water is poured, bread is broken, bodies are anointed, or vows are exchanged, the Spirit of God fills those participating with his heavenly grace. I am not sure anyone can fully grasp the power and beauty of the sacraments. Perhaps one of the reasons is that they are so unassuming and humble. Simple elements like water, bread, wine, and oil are used to sustain, heal, and transform us."[9]

Jesus said, "Behold, I make all things new" (Rv 21:5). The sacraments are the blessings of his new creation. The following table shows how the various sacraments bring about this process of transformation in union with HIM by *healing* our wounds, blessing our *identity*, and calling us to share in his *mission*. This table also serves as an overview for the next seven chapters.

Sacraments (of Christ)	Healing (of Wounds)	Identity (in Christ)	Mission (with Christ)
Baptism	Rejection	The Father's beloved	Imitating the Father's love
Holy Communion	Abandonment	Abiding presence	Incarnating Christ's presence
Confirmation	Powerlessness	Anointed with power	Ministering in the power of the Spirit
Holy Orders	Confusion	The Father's authority	Restoring holy authority
Matrimony	Fear	God's faithful love	Representing Christ's faithful love
Reconciliation	Shame	Pure and undefiled	Extending the Father's mercy
Anointing of the Sick	Hopelessness	Raised to life	Spreading Christ's hope and healing

Looking at the table from left to right, notice how the seven sacraments heal the seven deadly wounds and bring us into our true identity and mission in Christ.

In Baptism, we receive the Father's blessing through word and Spirit. This grace heals the wounds of rejection as we share in Jesus' identity as *the Father's beloved* and enables us to embody the Father's love to a world hungering for it.

In Holy Communion, Jesus' precious body and blood communicate his *abiding presence*, potentially healing the wounds of abandonment in us and in all of our relationships.

In Confirmation, we are *anointed with power* by the Holy Spirit to participate in Christ's mission to heal the wounds of powerlessness in ourselves and in those to whom we minister.

Through Holy Orders, a beloved son operates in his *Father's authority* to bless all who come to God in humble submission, thus healing the wounds of confusion and disorder that result from the world's rebellion.

In the sacrament of Matrimony, a man and woman become an image of *God's faithful love*, thereby overcoming wounds of fear and mistrust that have accumulated from broken relationships since the beginning of time.

In the sacrament of Reconciliation, a sinner is released from shame and healed from the effects of sin, becoming progressively more like Christ himself—*pure and undefiled*—while sharing in his ministry of reconciliation.

In the Anointing of the Sick, an infirm person is *raised to life* in Christ and given hope for his final resurrection from the dead, conquering the wounds of death and hopelessness.

Can you see how the sacraments heal us, restore our identity, and empower us by his Spirit to participate in Christ's mission (see *CCC*, 1210–1666)? All of this makes sense when we understand the purpose and power of God's blessing. His word and Spirit are poured out to us so that we can be brought back into intimate relationship through HIM.

Dr. Emoto's research helps us understand how this unfolds. Words spoken with conviction, in the power of the Spirit, are powerful forces for transformation. They create the reality they proclaim. If this is true of our human words, how much more so with God's life-giving words of blessing, which are living and actively creative? When received in faith with an open heart, God's blessings have the power to transform every aspect of our lives and fill us with God's divine life.

There is no limit to God's power. How can we not be blessed when we are in Christ and he is in us? St. Paul put it this way: "Yet I live, no longer I, but Christ lives in me" (Gal 2:20). He was not just speaking about his own identity and mission, but ours as well: "I myself am convinced about you, my brothers, that you yourselves are *full of goodness*" (Rom 15:14, emphasis added). That goodness inside of each one of us is the Holy Spirit, whom we receive and rely on daily in the sacraments. He alone is capable of forming the image of Christ in us. As long as we are willing to cooperate, the Holy Spirit is actively working in us, making us increasingly more whole and holy. Our response of faith—our yes, like Mary's fiat at the annunciation—is vitally important to receiving all the blessings that the Father desires to pour out to us.

The Father's generosity is amazing, isn't it? Let's take a moment to reflect on this so that we may each more fully appropriate these realities personally in our daily lives.

Take a Moment

1. Count your blessings! How has the Father blessed you through creation and through his sacraments? Identify a few specific ways.

2. Explain how Jesus' words create new realities. How is this power passed on through the sacraments of the Church?

3. Which of the seven deadly wounds are you most aware of in your life? Which of the identity lies listed in the table on page 26 has the strongest hold on your life?

4. As you review the table on page 30, which of the new identities in Christ are most visible in your life? What sacraments are associated with those identities?

—⟋⟍—

Scripture Meditation

The following passage from Ephesians 1 recounts many of the blessings we receive in Christ through the sacraments and prayer. Read this passage prayerfully three times, asking the Holy Spirit to reveal what he desires you to receive:

1. As you read it the first time, pay attention to the words or phrases that speak to your heart.

2. The second time through, read even more slowly and allow the Holy Spirit to highlight the sacraments implied in these specific blessings.

3. On the third time, read it very slowly, asking the Holy Spirit to show you how the Father desires to personally bless you now.

Blessed Are You

"Blessed be the God and Father of our Lord Jesus Christ, who has blessed us in Christ with every spiritual blessing in the heavens, as he chose us in him, before the foundation of the world, to be holy and without blemish before him. In love he destined us for adoption to himself through Jesus Christ, in accord with the favor of his will, for the praise of the glory of his grace that he granted us in the beloved" (Eph 1:3–6).

Let Us Pray

Pray the powerful words of Psalm 103 out loud, asking the Holy Spirit to enable you to bring joy to the Father's heart as you speak words of blessing in adoration of him, in an expression of gratitude for his great love and generosity toward you through the sacraments of Christ's redemption.

Bless the Lord

"Bless the LORD, my soul; all my being bless [your] holy name!
Bless the LORD, my soul; and do not forget all his gifts.
Who pardons all [my] sins, and heals all [my] ills, who redeems [my] life from the pit, and crowns [me] with mercy and compassion, who fills [my] days with good things, so [my] youth is renewed like the eagle's. . . .
Merciful and gracious is the LORD, slow to anger, abounding in mercy.
He will not always accuse, and nurses no lasting anger. . . .
Bless the LORD, all his creatures, everywhere in his domain.
Bless the LORD, my soul!" (Ps 103:1–5, 8–9, 22).

3

THE FATHER'S BELOVED

How Baptism Heals Wounds of Rejection

As the Father loves me, so I also love you.
Remain in my love.

John 15:9

"Every child a wanted child!" You may recognize this slogan as the rallying cry of the Planned Parenthood organization over many decades. I suspect it originated out of the life experience of its founder, Margaret Higgins Sanger. According to her biographers, Sanger grew up as the middle child in a family of eleven children. Her mother, a devout Catholic, died at the age of forty-nine. Sanger's father, though also a baptized Catholic, became increasingly antagonistic to Christianity throughout his life. Sanger's biographers report that he drank heavily, provided poorly for his family, and spent much of his time and energy railing against Christian morality.[1]

Watching her mother suffer through multiple miscarriages while caring for a large and growing family without her father's financial or emotional support must have been very difficult for the young Sanger. It is not hard to imagine that she saw herself as that prototypical overlooked child. Her biographers attest that Sanger's worldview was intrinsically shaped by her mother's premature death, which Sanger blamed on too many pregnancies and miscarriages. At her mother's funeral Sanger reportedly screamed at her father, "You caused this. Mother is dead from having too many children!"[2] You might think she would identify more with her mother, whom she loved. But instead Sanger, vowing to escape her mother's fate, followed in her father's footsteps, railing against all things sacred. Given her life experience as a child, she readily accepted the popular hysteria about overpopulation in the world and embraced eugenics, a philosophy that sought to eliminate the "unworthy" members of society in order to form a superior race.[3]

These insights from Sanger's childhood and young adult years make sense of her lifelong disdain for Christianity and her burning passion to "save" women and society from the burden of "unwanted" children. Both her personal life choices and her "missionary" work in establishing Planned Parenthood reveal her consuming zeal to prevent the birth of any child who she believed might be a burden to family or society. Additionally, she vowed to save every woman from what she considered the triple tyranny of faith, marriage, and childbearing.[4] Birth control and abortion were the preferred "sacraments" in Sanger's religion. Through her influence, they have become the practical religion throughout much of Western civilization.

Sanger's anti-gospel message, which St. John Paul II referred to as the "gospel of death," is not original to her. We might also refer to it as a "gospel of rejection." It actually started back at the beginning of time when Lucifer first rejected God's love and spread this cancerous wound of rejection throughout the world. After deceiving our first parents to mistrust the Father's love, he has been on a mission to "steal and slaughter and destroy" every life since (Jn 10:10).

At first glance, Sanger's motto of "every child a wanted child" sounds eerily similar to the teaching of the Church, but in reality it stands in direct opposition. Sanger's solution was to *reject* and eliminate any child *not wanted* by family or society. The Church, in contrast, values every human life and believes that every child is wanted and worthy of being welcomed into the world with love. Kimberly Hahn beautifully articulates the Church's position in a few succinct words: "Children are only and always a blessing. . . . They have value for their own sake because they are created by God in his image. Children are pure gift."[5]

In the Father's household, there are no unwanted children, only ones who have not yet realized their true dignity. In God's kingdom, *every child is a wanted child* because every single person is created by God and chosen in Christ from the foundation of the world (see Eph 1:4; *CCC*, 1077). In the Father's heart, there are no throwaway or disposable children, or adults for that matter. We are all wanted and have inestimable value because we are made in the image and likeness of our God, who is love (see 1 Jn 4:8).

The gospel of life and love is best exemplified by another woman, St. Teresa of Calcutta, who throughout her life and missionary work, reverenced the image of God in every person. Championing life, she cherished every person she encountered, giving special care to those whom the world would deem unfit and unwanted. Ultimately, she invited the outcasts and discarded of society to experience the intimate love of Jesus, leading many to receive their true dignity in the sacrament of Baptism. In St. Teresa's worldview, there truly were no unwanted children, only ones not yet fully blessed.[6]

Baptism is a public blessing declaring that you and I are precious and unrepeatable gifts of the Father. By restoring our relationship with God, Baptism fundamentally heals the wounds of rejection that have plagued the human race since our fall from grace. Though God never rejected Adam and Eve, their decision to reject him invited a curse of rejection into the world, which has infected all of humanity. Subsequently, every child born into this world is marked with an inherent deficiency due to original sin (see Rom 6; *CCC*, 396–398). Outside of Baptism we remain cut off from the Father's love and delight.

In Christ (through Baptism), this primordial curse of rejection is overcome as we receive the Father's blessing and are elevated to participate in his Trinitarian love. Thus begins the long journey of healing and reintegration, where the Holy Spirit, with our cooperation, restores us to wholeness and reestablishes our identity in the image of God. We become, as St. Paul says, "new creations" in Christ: "So whoever is in Christ is a new creation: the old things have passed away; behold, new things have come. And all this is from God, who has reconciled us to himself through Christ" (2 Cor 5:17–18).

In Baptism, we receive the blessing that the Father bestowed upon Jesus at his Baptism: "This is my beloved Son, with whom I am well pleased" (Mt 3:17). United with Christ, we become the Father's beloved in whom he delights. The same Holy Spirit who descended as a gift upon Jesus also comes to dwell in us. Through this supernatural rebirth, the Father pours out his love as pure gift, washing us clean (by the blood of Jesus and the symbol of water) of anything that would defile us and filling our hearts with his love. In this process of cleansing and regeneration, every baptized person is sealed as the Father's beloved child.

As the gateway to our life in the Spirit (see *CCC*, 1213), Baptism stands at the very center of the gospel of life and love, communicating into the depths of individual souls the supernatural graces flowing from Jesus' life, death, and resurrection. In this sacred rite, we are cleansed, signed, sealed, and delivered; rescued from the clutches of the evil one who would seek to kill and destroy us; and brought safely into the hands of our heavenly family (see Rom 8:16; Eph 1:3–14; 1 Jn 3:2; *CCC*, 1213, 1216, 1234, and 1279).

—⁂—

The grace of Baptism is beyond anything we can comprehend with our finite minds. But if you are like me, you feel the pain of the gap between this objective reality and most of our subjective experiences. How can we believe what the Church teaches is true when we don't see the full evidence of these realities within ourselves and in the world around us? If Baptism really is this powerful, and I believe it is, shouldn't our lives look more like Jesus'?

How can the same grace that enables Mother Teresa or John Paul II to become saints seem to have no discernible effect in others? Given the fact that we all objectively receive the same gift of the Holy Spirit at Baptism, how is it possible that some among us love and trust God while others live in radical opposition to their baptismal identity and calling, rejecting God altogether? Aren't beloved children called to be imitators of their Father (see Eph 5:1)? How is it possible for those who have been sealed by the Holy Spirit and delivered from evil to turn their backs and become imitators of the father of lies instead?

Judging strictly from the lives of many who are baptized, it is tempting to believe that Baptism is a silly superstition, just an empty and meaningless ritual with no real consequences. How do we reconcile all those who claim to be Christian yet are seduced instead by the spirit of the Antichrist? How do we reconcile the teaching of Jesus and his Church with the reality that many baptized people fail to live from their true identity as his beloved children?

As I have wrestled with this question myself, I have found insight in these words from Fr. Raniero Cantalamessa, the household preacher for the past three popes: "Catholic theology can help us understand how a sacrament can be valid and legal but 'unreleased' . . . if its fruit remains bound or unused. . . . Sacraments are not magic rites that act mechanically, without people's knowledge or collaboration. . . . The fruit of the sacrament depends wholly on divine grace, however this divine grace does not act without the 'yes'—the consent and affirmation—of the person."[7]

When I read Fr. Cantalamessa's explanation, it helped me understand how both St. Teresa of Calcutta and Margaret Sanger could be baptized as infants but with such different outcomes. Both were apparently given the gift of the Holy Spirit with all the accompanying supernatural graces, but of the two, it appears that only St. Teresa spent her life drawing on these graces by imitating her heavenly Father, sharing his love, and affirming the dignity of every person by seeing them as beloved sons and daughters of the Father. She basked in the radiance of the Father's bountiful love and participated in healing the wounds of rejection everywhere she went. Sanger, on the other hand, by all evidence, followed her human father's example, disdaining her Baptism and publicly rejecting Christ and his Church. In trying to "save" children and women from experiencing rejection, she instead promulgated the primordial wound of rejection throughout the world. It appears the graces of her Baptism remained "unreleased."

What does this say to you about the power of the sacrament of Baptism and what is necessary for us to live more fully in these graces?[8] Let's take a moment to reflect on this more deliberately.

Take a Moment

1. Do you believe you were a wanted child? Why or why not?
2. What do you believe happens when someone is baptized? What is our part in living the graces from our Baptism?

I wonder how Margaret Sanger would have answered these reflection questions. I seriously doubt that she saw her Baptism as anything other than an empty religious ritual or a confining yoke of slavery, especially later in her life. I can't imagine that she saw herself as a beloved daughter of the Father or that the reality of *good Father* even existed in her mind. How could she possibly see her own life as a gift when she saw others' lives as worthless or disposable? I wonder if she believed she was an unwanted child.

Though young Sanger was presumably baptized into the love of God by her parents, I doubt she knew much about God's love or her value in God's eyes. If she did, she must have rejected it at some point in her life out of her distorted images of God. History shows that she was not an "imitator of God" in what she taught or how she lived. Her path of "salvation" was in reality a path of destruction for many of her disciples who, like her, have their baptismal identity stolen from them by the father of lies.

In no way is this intended as a condemnation of Margaret Sanger the person but rather as an example of the dangers of rejecting our baptismal identity. As I write this, I pray that she might still fully receive God's mercy that was offered to her as an infant in Baptism.

Like many of us, I believe she was deceived into listening to the voice of the one who came to steal, kill, and destroy God's blessings (see Jn 10:10). At times in our lives, we have probably all been seduced by the father of lies and have been led down destructive paths.

Few of us are already mature in holiness like St. Teresa of Calcutta or St. John Paul II. If we are honest with ourselves, we can acknowledge that we love God and others poorly much of the time. Too many of us still have to contend with significant wounds of rejection in our lives, and though we don't want to acknowledge it, these wounds still cause damage to others through us. Of all the internal monsters that terrify us, rejection (believing that we are unloved and unlovable) is among the worst. *The feeling of rejection is an experience of hell.* Most of us will do almost anything to save ourselves and those around us from this trauma.

Donna, a woman I prayed with during a healing service, is a prime example of how our unhealed wounds can cause us to unwittingly wound ourselves and others. Conversely, her healing process is a beautiful reminder of our baptismal inheritance as beloved children of the Father, showing how his merciful love heals the wounds of rejection in us and enables us to spread his love to others.

Brought up in a good Christian family, one where faith remained centrally important, Donna received the sacrament of Baptism as an infant. Her parents took seriously their responsibility of bringing her up in the faith. Donna's religious practices remained important to her even during the many years she felt alienated from God and unworthy of his love. A profound moment of grace came during a healing service when she reached out for the Father's mercy. After going to confession for the first time in twenty years and receiving the Lord's forgiveness, the priest encouraged her to receive extra prayer for healing.

Donna made her way to the back of the church and tapped me on the shoulder. Before she could say a word to me about what was wrong, she burst into tears. Drawing close enough so that no one else could hear what she was about to say, she whispered: "I have had three abortions. I just went to confession and the priest told me to find you for more prayer."

Nearly Donna's entire adult life had been overshadowed by this oppressive secret and accompanying guilt and self-hatred that haunted her every day of her life. My heart broke for her and for her aborted children as she recounted how she had suffered personally and unwittingly caused these innocent children horrific suffering. Though she had been objectively forgiven by the priest in confession, she told me she could not receive God's mercy, nor could she ever forgive herself.

I knew that none of my words could penetrate the fortress of her self-contempt, which was keeping torrents of pain and horror buried deep inside her heart. After finding a quiet space where she could share freely, I asked her if we could pray. When she consented, we together asked the Holy Spirit to reveal to us whatever he wanted Donna to know.

After several minutes of silence in listening prayer, I could see Donna's facial expressions relax as she seemed to be receiving new insights from the Holy Spirit. When she was ready, she began to speak these revelations out loud:

> I now understand why I did what I did. I have felt rejected my entire life. I don't know why. My parents are loving people, but I could never believe they loved me or that I was loveable. Somehow my mother's angry outbursts early in my life left me feeling like I was not wanted from the very beginning. I also don't think she was ready for me when she got pregnant. I always felt like I was a burden to her.
>
> When I became pregnant the first time as a teenager, my first thought was that "everyone will reject me when they find out." I feared my mother's reaction the most. But I said to myself, "That is no reason to have an abortion." I knew it was wrong. Then a second

thought came, that convinced me I had to *protect* this baby inside me from feeling rejected all her life because she would be "illegitimate." I couldn't bear the thought of her going through her whole life feeling the way I have. I had to save her from that. When I got pregnant again in my twenties and a third time in my thirties, I knew I had to "protect" these children in the same way. What difference did it make if I had more abortions? I knew I could never undo the first one, and my life was already ruined.

Donna continued:

Now that I am seeing everything clearly, I can't believe how blind I was to what was really going on. Those babies were God's gifts entrusted to me to love and nurture even though I was not following God's will at the time. Can you believe what I did? In trying to prevent them from feeling rejected, I completely rejected them and kept them from ever knowing they were loved and accepted by anyone.

At this point, Donna's tears turned into deep sobs as she faced the truth of what she had done. She seemed horrified as she described to me images of her babies as they were being rejected in the womb. After releasing years of deeply held pain, Donna shared more conviction from the Holy Spirit:

Somehow I thought I was guarding my children from feeling that same pain I felt . . . but how awful, I didn't really protect them—I hurt them. I didn't want them to feel "unwanted," but then in the end I treated them like they were totally unwanted not only by the rest of the world but especially by me. I am their mother, and I rejected them way more than my mom ever rejected

me. I didn't want them to be a burden in my life. . . .
Oh no, I am so much worse than my mother!

At this point I sensed that I needed to stop Donna because she was now twisting the Holy Spirit's liberating insights and turning them into more ammunition for self-rejection. Perceiving the father of lies trying to steal her healing, I asked her if we could pray again. After receiving her consent, we began asking the Holy Spirit to heal these wounds of rejection, both in Donna's life and in the lives of her unborn, aborted babies.

Over the next twenty minutes, Donna's sorrow turned into an overflowing joy as the Father quieted his precious daughter in his love. In the sanctuary of her heart, the Holy Spirit led Donna through the process of healing her wounds and releasing her shame and guilt. He began by bringing her back to the moment of her Baptism as an infant and showing her how the Father loved and accepted her before she could do anything good or bad. He showed her that original sin was washed away at her Baptism, not because she earned it but because of Jesus' sacrifice on the cross. He pointed out that her confession was a renewing of these baptismal graces.[9] Jesus atoned for her sin because he loved her.

The Holy Spirit further revealed to Donna that Jesus' death on the cross was similar to an abortion. He was pierced and bled; his innocent life was cut off by others who were deceived by the evil one. They were acting out of their own fears and rejection wounds. If Jesus could forgive those people who rejected and aborted his life, he could certainly forgive her. (After these insights, Donna reported that she was able to receive God's mercy and forgiveness. We walked through a simple prayer together so she could actively forgive herself and ask her babies to forgive her. After our vocal prayer, she responded with deep healing sobs, releasing more of the self-rejection, sorrow, and guilt she had been carrying.)

As we continued listening in prayer, Donna realized that her parents were actually delighted to have her as their little girl when she was conceived, even if they were not completely ready for her birth.

She saw that her mother's anger was not because Donna was unlovable or a burden but that it came out of her mother's own frustrations, wounds, and sins. (At this point Donna felt compelled to stop and forgive her mother; when she finished forgiving, her face lit up with a big smile.)

Finally, the Holy Spirit prompted Donna to offer her children to Jesus (see Mk 10:14; *CCC*, 1261). As Donna offered each child to Jesus, she began to laugh with great joy and relief, trusting for the first time that her babies were safe, no longer rejected or forsaken but forever loved and cherished in heaven where they would one day be reunited with her and her parents. As Donna spoke, I thought of the scripture passage, "See what love the Father has bestowed on us that we may be called the children of God. Yet so we are" (1 Jn 3:1).

As we finished our prayer, Donna and I each blessed the Father with a heartfelt prayer of thanksgiving, grateful that we had been blessed to participate in this mystery of redemption, one that began in each of our lives at Baptism. Now as imitators of the Father, we were given the honor of interceding for her unborn and unbaptized children, who, after all this time, did not have to live as rejected or unwanted children but could receive the blessing of the Father as his beloved sons and daughters. We simply did what the Church teaches for all unbaptized children: "With respect to children who have died without baptism, the liturgy of the Church invites us to trust in God's mercy and to pray for their salvation" (*CCC*, 1283).

Donna's story illustrates how vulnerable we are to turning away from our heavenly Father even though he has joined us to Christ and calls us his beloved children. Though we have the Holy Spirit to guide us, there is another spirit in the world actively trying to destroy us and to lead us to reject God, ourselves, and his ways of love (see 1 Jn 4:1–6). As the Church and scripture teach so clearly, we are in a real battle for our souls (see 1 Pt 5:8–10; *CCC*, 2725, 2850–2854). How do we keep from being deceived by the father of lies and losing sight of our true identity?

St. Ignatius of Loyola provided a great tool for baptized believers to discern these spirits in his *Spiritual Exercises*.[10] In the exercises, Ignatius identifies two opposing spirits that he says are always at work in our lives and in the world. He simply calls them the "good spirit" (which represents our hearts attuned to the Holy Spirit) and the "evil spirit" (which refers to our fallen human nature influenced by the father of lies and subject to the world's influences).

Does it make sense to you that even though they were each baptized and given the gift of the Holy Spirit both Margaret Sanger and Donna allowed the evil spirit to deceive them? I don't believe that either of these women actively set out to be accomplices of the evil spirit in stealing, killing, or destroying human life. Rather, like Eve, I believe they were first seduced and then deceived by the father of lies into believing that what they were doing was something good or at least necessary. Isn't that the case with us most of the time?

The evil spirit is obviously acting behind the scenes in the act of abortion (which is just a modern version of child sacrifice) as well as in the philosophies that undergird the culture of death. But they are certainly not the only manifestations of the evil spirit. Rejection, which is the fruit of sin, is all around us and inside us. Taking hold in us and in our relationships, the spirit of rejection chokes out the love Jesus promised us (see Rom 5:12, Jn 10:10).

Whenever any aspect of our life, our joy, or our true identity is thwarted or aborted in some way, we can be assured that the enemy of our souls is working to plant seeds of rejection. The evil one, who is eternally rejected, seeks to bring us into his misery. When those seeds are received into the ground of our souls, eventually they become firm roots of rejection, effectively choking out the life God planted in us through Baptism (see Mt 12:22, 37; 13:18–29).

The evil spirit, who is himself condemned, tries to bring us under the same condemnation so that we hate and reject ourselves (see Jn 12:31, 16:11). As Henri Nouwen observed, this is deadly to our spiritual life: "Self-rejection is the greatest enemy of the spiritual life because it contradicts the sacred voice that calls us the 'beloved.' Being the beloved constitutes the core truth of our existence."[11]

Donna knew what she did was wrong, but rather than trust in God's forgiveness as a beloved daughter, she felt like an outcast, forever condemned for her abortions. She came into agreement with the curses of the evil spirit by condemning and hating herself, reinforcing her already deep wound of rejection. The deception from the evil spirit led her to believe that God had rejected her. But Jesus makes it very clear that the Father does not condemn us or reject us: "For God did not send his Son into the world to condemn the world, but that the world might be saved through him" (Jn 3:17); "I ask, then, has God rejected his people? Of course not! . . . For the gifts and the call of God are irrevocable" (Rom 11:1, 29). God is not the one who condemns us; we condemn ourselves by staying in the darkness of our sin and denying his mercy (see Jn 3:17–21; Rom 8:1, 33–35).

This is why Baptism is one of God's primary weapons against the tactics of our adversary. It is an infusion of God's love into our hearts and an objective marker that proclaims we have been sealed as the Father's beloved. Always remember you are the beloved child in whom your Father delights; you are marked and sealed in the name of the living God, who now lives inside you. You are a new creation in Christ, living not for yourself but for the glory of God, called to love others as he has loved you. In this way you have been called to heal the primordial wound of rejection that prevents all of us from believing in and receiving God's love.

Let's take a moment and reflect on Donna's experiences and all of ours to see how the Holy Spirit may want to speak to each one of us about this battle we are engaged in. Then, in the following scripture meditation and prayer, I invite you to let these realities penetrate the depths of your heart.

Take a Moment

1. In what ways have you felt rejected? How do you reject yourself?

2. What role did Baptism play in Donna's healing? How did prayer and God's Word help in the process of her restoration?

3. Describe the opposing spirits behind abortion and Baptism. Where do you recognize the battle between these spiritual realities in your life?

Scripture Meditation

1. Pray and ask the Holy Spirit to lead you in reflecting on this scripture passage.

2. Read this passage three times slowly, listening to the words or phrases that the Holy Spirit is revealing to you.

3. After each time write down or discuss what speaks to your heart.

The Father's Beloved

"See what love the Father has bestowed on us that we may be called the children of God. Yet so we are. The reason the world does not know us is that it did not know him. Beloved, we are God's children now; what we shall be has not yet been revealed. We do know that when it is revealed, we shall be like him, for we shall see him as he is. Everyone who has this hope based on him makes himself pure, as he is pure" (1 Jn 3:1–3).

Let Us Pray

Begin by asking the Holy Spirit to guide you. Then slowly bless yourself, in the name of the Father (who is love), the Son (who is the beloved), and the Holy Spirit (who is the bond of love). As you make the Sign of the Cross on your body, you are renewing your baptismal blessing. As you do this, remember Jesus' death on the cross, which enabled you to become the Father's beloved son or daughter at Baptism; he is continuing to bless you with those graces now with your cooperation. Let your heart ponder these realities.

Notice that the words of the Apostles' (and Nicene) Creed are summarized in the renewal of our baptismal vows that are normally spoken with the entire Church during Easter. They can be spoken at any time. Speak these words slowly and with conviction:

> I renounce Satan (the father of lies).
> I renounce all his works (sin).
> I renounce all his empty promises (deceptions).
> I believe in God, the Father almighty, (who out of his great love is) the Creator of heaven and earth.
> I believe in Jesus Christ, his only Son, our Lord, who (out of his great desire to express the Father's love to humanity) was born of the Virgin Mary, was crucified, died, and was buried, rose from the dead, and is now seated at the right hand of the Father.
> I believe in the Holy Spirit, (whose powerful bond of love is embodied in) the holy Catholic Church, the Communion of Saints, the forgiveness of sins, the resurrection of the body, and life everlasting.

Renouncing the works of Satan and affirming our faith in God can take place every day and every moment of our lives. We are given this authority by virtue of our Baptism. Let's put this into practice: Suppose someone said something that offended you, and you are left feeling rejected. Try praying the following:

> In the name and authority of Jesus Christ, which I received in my Baptism, I renounce the lie that I am not loved or loveable.
> I renounce the curse of rejection that comes from the father of lies.
> I renounce the authority that I have given to anyone else but you, Father, to tell me my value and

worth. You, Father, are the only one who completely knows me and loves me as I am.

I acknowledge that by virtue of my Baptism, I am loved and delighted in by you, Father.

I also acknowledge that, by virtue of my blessing in Baptism, you have given me your Holy Spirit, whose love is poured out into my heart.

I am one with Jesus, your beloved. Amen.

4

ABIDING PRESENCE

How Holy Communion Heals
Wounds of Abandonment

Whoever eats my flesh and drinks my blood
remains in me and I in him.

John 6:56

Growing up in a large family, I don't remember feeling alone until I turned thirteen years old. That is when my dad left our family and moved to another city, and my underlying sense of security went out the door with him. During the day, I could keep my mind active with school, sports, friends, entertainment, and family interactions. But when I went to bed at night, I couldn't escape the pervasive feeling of loneliness. *I missed my dad terribly.*

For the first time in my life, I felt unprotected. At night, every little noise scared me. I would naively pull the covers up over my face so that a robber wouldn't see me if he broke into our house. But worse than these fears was an insidious sense of emptiness that permeated my soul. Back then, I couldn't have expressed what I was feeling. That would come years later after months of therapy and some healing experiences enabled me to finally grieve the loss of my dad at such a vulnerable age.

You, too, no doubt have felt the pain of abandonment in your life in some form or fashion. There could be any number of reasons why: the death of a loved one; broken friendships; not being protected in an abusive situation; or perhaps, like me, you, too, experienced the heartbreak of divorce in your family. These are obvious experiences

51

of abandonment. But the wound of abandonment can be manifested in more subtle ways as well, such as feeling alone in a crowd, not being understood for who you are, not receiving the affection or comfort you need, or experiencing yourself on the outside of community life.

The manifestations may be many, but underneath all of these separations is this primordial wound of abandonment that entered our human experience with original sin. On this side of Eden, all of us know what it is like to feel alone, unprotected, and cut off from intimacy in our vital relationships. During these times, we may even wonder if anyone cares, including God. Frequently, these abandonment wounds get transferred into our relationship with our heavenly Father. Though he promised that he would never leave or forsake us (see Heb 13:5), our hearts have difficulty trusting the reality of God's presence. When my dad left, God seemed far away to me, too. Perhaps you can relate.

Whether we are conscious of experiencing the pain of abandonment or not, it is an inevitable part of our human experience in this fallen world. Ever since that first sin, our relationships with God and one another have been fractured. We live in a world where separation and disconnection are the norm. Many of us can't identify the feeling of abandonment because it is all we have ever known. We think this is "just the way life is." We get used to feeling disconnected in our families, at church, and in our daily activities. It just seems normal.

Though it may be part of our current reality, it is not what God intended for us from the beginning or the reality he desires for us now and in the future. The *Catechism*, basing itself on sacred scripture, affirms that we are made for intimate communion with God and one another: "God himself is an eternal exchange of love, Father, Son, and Holy Spirit, and he has destined us to share in that exchange" (*CCC*, 221).

In the beginning, Adam and Eve mirrored and participated in the most holy communion of the blessed Trinity. They also enjoyed a profound intimacy with one another, which St. John Paul II refers to as "original unity."¹ In their unbroken bond of love, they did not know the experience of loneliness or abandonment. They experienced God's abiding presence with them at all times.

Whether we are conscious of it or not, deep down each one of us yearns for this kind of holy intimacy because it is written into the fabric of our being. The psalmist expresses this longing with poetic beauty: "My soul thirsts for God, the living God" (Ps 42:3). And the saints know of this yearning as well. After years of trying to fill his void in all the wrong places, St. Augustine finally turned his heart to the only real source of his fulfillment. Do you recognize this longing for a greater measure of God's presence in your own heart? In heaven it will be completely fulfilled. But we don't have to wait to experience it. We can enter into communion with him now. The Church teaches that this is why Jesus gave us the sacrament of his presence as a means for us to continually abide in him: "The principle fruit of receiving the Eucharist in Holy Communion is an intimate union with Christ Jesus. Indeed, the Lord said: 'He who eats my flesh and drinks my blood *abides* in me and I in him'" (*CCC*, 1391, emphasis added). St. John Paul II adds, "The Eucharist is the sacrament of the presence of Christ, who gives himself to us because he loves us. He loves each one of us in a unique way in our practical daily lives."²

St. Luke's account from the book of Acts gives us a flavor of how the sacrament of Holy Communion was practiced in the early Church. The apostles lived the reality of Christ's abiding presence with them and allowed his presence to permeate their community life: "They devoted themselves to the teaching of the apostles and to communal life, to the breaking of the bread and to the prayers" (Acts 2:42). "The community of believers was of one heart and mind, and no one claimed that any of his possessions was his own, but they had everything in common. With great power the apostles bore witness to the resurrection of the Lord Jesus, and great favor was accorded them all" (Acts 4:32–33).

Most of these activities from the early Church are still common in our worship: the apostles' teaching (God's word in the scripture), the breaking of bread (the sacrament of Holy Communion), and prayer (invoking God's presence and intercession for others). But one element is largely missing in many of our churches—"communal life." The original in the Greek is *koinonia*, which when translated into English, means "communion" or "fellowship." While we have some small degree of fellowship in our modern communities, it is still a far cry from what the early Church practiced. Can we honestly say that most of us are "devoted to communal life" to the degree that the early disciples appeared to be? Can we say we are "one heart and mind" and that our belongings are not our own but are for the good of our brothers and sisters? Can this be one of the reasons we are not witnessing the "great power" of Jesus' resurrection as they did?

Is it naive to expect these things in our large, modern churches? The *Catechism* provides the answer by reminding us the sacrament of Holy Communion is a participation (koinonia) in heavenly worship (see *CCC*, 1326). Are we cognizant of participating with the hosts of heaven when we worship together? It also calls this sacrament "a bond of charity" and "a sign of unity" (*CCC*, 1323). Within ourselves and our communities, are we really operating in unity like the early Church; can most of us say we are experiencing authentic communion (koinonia)? Why then do we call this sacrament Holy Communion when these most essential elements are neglected in our worship and community life?

The problem is obviously not on Jesus' end. His real presence in the Eucharist truly does bring the reality of heaven to earth. His body and blood are the source of our charity and unity. Giving himself completely to us, he makes us one body with him and with one another. Yet how many of us daily embody this reality of Jesus' abiding presence? Our wounds of abandonment and sins of isolation and selfishness seem to get in the way of true fellowship (koinonia), first in relationship with Jesus and then with one another.

—◊—

The scriptures and Church teaching, as well as our own experiences, confirm that there can be no genuine unity or communion without self-giving love. In the words of St. John Paul II, "To celebrate the Eucharist, 'to eat his flesh and drink his blood,' means to accept the wisdom of the cross and the path of service. It means that we signal our willingness to sacrifice ourselves for others, as Christ has done."[3]

In his insightful book *Life of the Beloved*, Henri Nouwen offers a vision of what self-sacrificing love looks like as we actively practice the sacrament of Holy Communion in our daily lives. Just as Jesus took the bread (as his body), blessed it, broke it, and gave it to his disciples at the Last Supper, he calls us to follow his example in Holy Communion (see Mt 26:26). When we offer ourselves as living sacrifices in worship (see Rom 12:1), Jesus also "takes us," "blesses us," "breaks us," and "gives us" so that we can participate with him in his holy self-offering.

Notice the sequence of events. First, Jesus *takes us* and makes us an eternal offering to the Father, with himself. We are reminded that our lives do not belong to us (see 1 Cor 6:19, Rom 14:8). We were given to the Father in Baptism. Every time we celebrate Holy Communion, we are invited to reaffirm the reality that we are one with Jesus and an integral part of his body, the Church.

After taking us into his hands, Jesus then *blesses us*. Blessing, as we have already noted, is receiving the presence and grace of God in our lives. When we receive him in Holy Communion, Jesus sanctifies us and makes us holy. We in turn bless him with our praise and thanksgiving (see *CCC*, 1078). In the Eucharist, which literally means "great thanksgiving," we become a thanksgiving offering in communion with Jesus. He blesses us so that we can share his presence with others. But first we need to be broken.

Following the blessing, Jesus *breaks us*. This is the part most of us want to avoid. I can personally testify. The breaking process is not always easy or fun, but neither was the cross for Jesus. Without the breaking of our pride and self-sufficiency, we cannot have unity or true communion (koinonia) with Jesus or one another.

Finally, after Jesus takes us, blesses us, and breaks us, he *gives us* as a gift to the Father for the good of others. His abiding presence flowing in and through our brokenness becomes a healing remedy to all we encounter. Individually and corporately we become the living Body of Christ, bringing the reality of Jesus' presence to a hungry and lonely world.

Taking, blessing, breaking, and giving—this is what it means for us to authentically celebrate Holy Communion with Jesus. Anything less is to fail to recognize Jesus' body (in the blessed bread, in the community, and in ourselves) (see 1 Cor 11).

—◊◊◊—

Examining ourselves through the mirror of scripture (especially Acts 2 and 4 and 1 Corinthians 11), we can see how many of us remain far from living in the fullness of the sacrament. But these scriptures also provide hope for us and our communities. We, too, are invited into the same Holy Communion with Jesus and our communities. But first we must let go of possessing our false comforts. We are all prone, to one degree or another, to hold on to our life, our possessions, our time, and our energy. The inevitable fruit of this selfishness is disconnection and disunity. We see the evidence everywhere, with more than fifty thousand different Christian denominations divided over the name of Jesus. This lack of unity in the overall Body of Christ flows into *every* church community and family. Many of our churches, families, and communities look a lot like the rest of the world—disconnected and fragmented. No wonder there are so many lonely and lost people in the world and in our churches.

In the early Church, when people offered themselves to Jesus, they also offered everything that belonged to them. Their property and possessions were freely offered for the benefit of everyone in need. It was an integral part of their worship. This same pattern we see in the book of Acts continued for hundreds of years following Jesus' resurrection. In studying Church history, I discovered that this prac-tice of sharing the necessities of life with one another continued on for several hundred years when Christians came together to celebrate Holy Communion. At their "love feasts" they gave food and clothing to those in need and then delivered it to those in the surrounding regions.

I doubt they rushed home to shop, lay on the couch to watch football, or spent their Sundays working in the yard. Instead, they went out together as one body in Christ, giving their time, energy, and possessions so that others could realize that God cared about them intimately and would "never leave or forsake them." They incarnated the reality they had earlier received in Holy Communion—his body and blood remained in them, and they conveyed his living presence to the world around them. They became, in a very sacramental way, his broken body and poured-out blood for a hungry and thirsty world.

In contrast, many of us today throw a few dollars into the collection basket and hardly know more than a handful of people in our community. Many of us come and go to church as though we are punching the clock at work, just putting in our time and fulfilling our obligation. It must break Jesus' heart over and over again to experience the contrast between his total self-gift and our pervasive self-centeredness. No wonder we have so little fellowship and feel alone so much of the time. Even at church, the place where we say we go to celebrate Holy Communion (koinonia), many of us remain strangers. Most of our communities don't look much like the Church in the book of Acts.

I don't believe this is how Jesus intended for us to live his abiding presence in the sacrament of Holy Communion. What has been your experience? Let's pause a moment to reflect.

Take a Moment

1. When and how have you experienced the pain of abandonment in your life?

2. How has Christian community either reinforced or healed those
   wounds?

3. What do you believe was present in the early Church community
   that is missing today in our communities?

—⟋⟍—

When I consider what may have contributed to the vibrancy of those
early Church communities, many things come to mind. I think about
how the apostles heard Jesus personally proclaim, "My flesh is true
food, and my blood is true drink" (Jn 6:55). They were confronted
right then with his literal meaning of those words as he challenged
them to leave if they didn't believe his teaching.

Later, I envision them celebrating the Passover meal before his
bloody sacrifice on Calvary, watching him closely as he took the
bread, blessed it, broke it, and gave it to them, saying, "Take, eat; this
is my body." I wonder what they felt when they received the cup from
Jesus' own hands and heard him speak these words: "Drink from it,
all of you, for this is my blood of the covenant, which will be shed on
behalf of many for the forgiveness of sins" (Mt 26:26–28).

It surely would take them several days before they would understand the meaning of these powerful words and gestures. Only after
enduring the anguish of his passion and death, and then touching his
resurrected body with their own hands, could these words make sense.
They surely would not treat his body and blood casually or with the
kind of indifference many of us often do.

Though most of them abandoned Jesus during his darkest hour,
and also probably felt abandoned by God during that entire nightmare,
they heard his promise that he would never forsake them (see Jn
14:18). Even if they didn't comprehend at first, they would eventually
come to understand that Jesus was promising to be with them in the
person of the Holy Spirit and in a particular way in the sacrament of
Holy Communion every time they gathered to remember his passion,
death, and resurrection.

When they "broke bread" in remembrance of his death and resurrection after Pentecost, these early disciples experienced the risen Jesus. His abiding presence filled their hearts and permeated their communities. Witnessing his resurrection power in their midst, healing and miracles abounded. By all evidence, these men, women, and children were on fire with the Holy Spirit. With their passionate zeal, they set the world around them ablaze with his love. Through them, people saw and experienced a living Jesus, not a faint memory of him. Carrying his divine presence, they attracted thousands into the Church.

This can still be true today as Jesus desires his Body, the Church, to be the primary place where we encounter his presence so we can, in turn, bring his love to the world around us. Isn't this what Pope Francis wants us to understand? "We can ask ourselves this question: When will we meet Jesus—only at the end? No, no, no. We meet him every day. But how? In prayer. When you pray, you meet Jesus. When you take Communion, you meet Jesus in the sacrament. . . . This meeting happens in prayer, when we go to Mass, and when we do good works: when we visit the sick, when we help the poor, when we think of others."[4]

This understanding of Jesus' abiding presence within the context of the sacraments and prayer is a major focus of our teaching and activities at the John Paul II Healing Center. During our conferences, we often provide demonstrations and prayer experiences that underscore the reality of abiding with the Trinity. Recently, during one of our conferences for priests, we had the privilege of praying with a few of the priests in attendance, inviting them to experience Jesus' presence in the places where they had previously only known the pain of abandonment.

I had the privilege of praying with Fr. Edward, who had a debilitating physical condition that prevented him from lifting his arms over his head. He lived with constant pain in his hands, shoulders, and arms. In our prayer time together, the Holy Spirit revealed to us that his physical ailment originated in unhealed abandonment wounds from early childhood experiences. Suffering for more than forty years, he had reached a crisis point and was desperate for help as these wounds continued crippling his priestly vocation, making it especially difficult to celebrate Mass.

My prayer time with Fr. Edward turned out to be much more intense than either of us anticipated. It reminded me that the *Catechism* describes contemplative prayer as an "intense time of prayer" where we encounter Jesus and he encounters us in the depths of our hearts (*CCC*, 2709–2719). Jesus met Fr. Edward in the depths of his heart and touched his deepest wounds. As we asked the Holy Spirit to reveal the root issues of Fr. Edward's ailment, he brought him in touch with early childhood memories of abandonment. He sobbed as he relived the searing pain of feeling cut off from both his mother and father's love and nurturing during early childhood. These early separations had left pervasive wounds in young Edward's soul, which eventually manifested in the debilitating effects in his body.

In prayer, the Holy Spirit showed him that the pain in his hands and arms reflected his longing to reach out to be held by his parents and that his shoulder pain revealed the burdens he carried in feeling responsible for everyone around him. He felt totally alone in the memory, but Jesus revealed to him that he was present with him in his childhood suffering and that he would now carry the burdens with him in the priesthood. As Jesus spoke these realities within the depths of Fr. Edward's heart, the pain in his hands, arms, and shoulders immediately began to decrease, and he was able to lift his arms partway over his head. But the healing was far from finished. Jesus invited him to continue the healing process within the celebration of the Eucharist, which was to take place immediately following our prayer time together.

Celebrating Mass as a community with the other priests and our team, Fr. Edward found his heart fully engaged in every part of the celebration. He later reported to all of us that after receiving Jesus in Communion, he experienced a warm and loving presence in his heart, which permeated throughout his entire body. As he felt Jesus' presence, he also heard Jesus tell him, "You are not alone. I am always with you."

Previous to this experience, Fr. Edward accepted these realities in faith, but after his prayer time, he could literally feel Jesus' presence with him after receiving the Eucharist. By the end of the *third day* of the conference (note the resurrection imagery), he was almost entirely pain-free from these ailments, which had been a source of constant pain throughout his life and a constant hindrance to his ministry. Sharing deeply in Jesus' sufferings on the cross, Fr. Edward now felt the joy of his resurrection life. All of us present shared in his exuberance as he lifted his arms in adoration and thanksgiving. (Prior to this he could not lift his arms over his head at all.)

Several months after attending the conference, Fr. Edward wrote to tell me that the fruits of his healing continued to be a source of joyful communion with the Trinity and the people he serves:

> Here we are, months after our retreat, and my experience of the Father's (and Jesus') love continues to deepen. At times my heart overflows with gratitude and compassion, especially as I share that love with those I serve. I remember mentioning at the retreat that my deep prayer during my ordination to the priesthood was to minister with the heart of the Father. I didn't know how that prayer would be answered, or even what that kind of ministry looked like, but now I see that prayer being realized. . . . Thank you for leading me deeper into the heart of the Father. What a blessing! What a life!

After reading Fr. Edward's testimony I began to wonder why Jesus' real presence in Holy Communion did not heal Fr. Edward before that moment on the retreat. Jesus certainly could have healed him at any time.[5] And I know Fr. Edward prayed for healing many times before coming to the conference. But after praying about this, the Holy Spirit showed me that there were obstacles in Fr. Edward's heart that needed to be addressed before he could receive the grace. Fr. Thomas Keating offers valuable insight regarding how these obstacles can be removed through contemplative prayer, freeing our hearts to become more receptive to Jesus' abiding presence in Holy Communion:

> The Eucharist received in Holy Communion awakens us to the permanent presence of Christ within us at the deepest level. The Eucharist, like the Word of God in scripture, has its primary purpose to bring us to the awareness of God's abiding presence within us. . . . Contemplative prayer reduces the obstacles to the transforming energy of the Eucharist, so that we can manifest in our attitudes and behavior the living Christ within us. . . . If we do not have a discipline to reduce the obstacles in us to experiencing the presence of God, the full power of the sacraments are diluted and do not achieve their full potential to transform us.[6]

These are important words for all of us to hear and take to heart. If we do not remove the obstacles, "the full power of the sacraments are diluted and do not achieve the potential to transform us." We all, I believe, have many obstacles that keep us from receiving the full grace of Holy Communion. Fr. Keating is simply affirming what the Church has always taught. The sacraments, in themselves, are powerful blessings, but all of us need to dispose and prepare our hearts to receive their full effects in our lives (see *CCC*, 1098). Contemplative prayer is an excellent way to dispose our hearts, allowing us to become more receptive, with a greater capacity for unity and charity.

Without the proper disposition of our hearts and communal unity and connectedness, our way of living out the sacrament of Holy Communion can too easily become an anti-witness, lacking charity, creating more disunity, and intensifying wounds of abandonment in us and in our families and communities. On the other hand, every authentic celebration and reception of Holy Communion fosters greater unity and charity, bringing us ever more deeply into communion with Jesus and with the "communion of saints" and thus healing these primordial wounds of abandonment that plague all of us in one way or another.

May all of us continually hunger and thirst for a greater intimacy with Jesus, knowing that the bond of communion that unites us to him and to one another is so much more real and satisfying than any false intimacy the world has to offer. I invite you now to personally apply all we have discussed.

Take a Moment

1. What are the barriers in your heart and community that prevent Jesus' abiding presence from being manifested more fully?

2. What are your thoughts and reactions to Fr. Edward's healing experience?

3. Recall any intense encounters you have had with Jesus in prayer or in the sacrament of Holy Communion. Describe what happened.

4. Consider how the process of "taking, blessing, breaking, and giving" occurred in the apostles' lives beginning with the Last Supper and proceeding into the early Church after Pentecost. How does this process play out in your life?

Scripture Meditation

The following passage from Acts 2 is a description of Holy Communion in the early Church immediately following Pentecost. Ask the Holy Spirit to guide you as you reflect on the scripture passage.

1. Read the passage slowly the first time through for overall understanding.

2. Read a second time slowly, listening to a word or phrase that stands out.

3. Read a third time very slowly, allowing the Holy Spirit to speak to you through the passage. Record what you receive.

Holy Communion in the Early Church

"They devoted themselves to the teaching of the apostles and to the communal life, to the breaking of the bread and to the prayers. Awe came upon everyone, and many wonders and signs were done through the apostles. All who believed were together and had all things in common; they would sell their property and possessions and divide them among all according to each one's need. Every day they devoted themselves to meeting together in the Temple area and to breaking bread in their homes. They ate their meals with exultation and sincerity of heart, praising God and enjoying favor with all the people. And every day the Lord added to their number those who were being saved" (Acts 2:42–47).

Let Us Pray

"Immanuel" means "God is with us." It is one of the names of Jesus given through the prophet Isaiah, signifying God's abiding presence with us. This real presence is what we celebrate in the sacrament of Holy Communion. The following prayer process could be prayed immediately after Communion, during adoration, or during any personal prayer time of your choosing.[7]

Begin by remembering God's promise: "I will never forsake you or abandon you" (Heb 13:5). Then quietly reflect upon these scriptures:

• "This is my body, which will be given for you" (Lk 22:19).

- "Whoever eats my flesh and drinks my blood remains in me and I in him" (Jn 6:56).

- "I am with you always, until the end of the age" (Mt 28:20).

- "I will not leave you orphans; I will come to you" (Jn 14:18).

- "I stand at the door and knock. If anyone . . . opens the door, I will enter his house and dine with him, and he with me" (Rv 3:20).

Practice Abiding in God's Presence

1. Be attentive to Jesus' presence currently or remember a time when you were especially aware of his presence.

2. Allow yourself to enter into the experience again now (the real meaning of "remembrance" is to live it again in the present moment).

3. Ask the Holy Spirit to bring to light a time when you felt alone.

4. Allow yourself to enter into that memory again—feeling it in the present moment. Experience the painful emotions.

5. Reconnect with the experience of Jesus' presence and ask the Holy Spirit to reveal his presence during this time you felt alone.

6. Record what he reveals to you (in a thought, memory, feeling, or image).

7. Thank Jesus for his presence and ask for his presence to remain with you as you leave the prayer experience. Stay in touch with his abiding presence during the day, every day.

5

ANOINTED WITH POWER

How Confirmation Heals Wounds of Powerlessness

You will receive power when the Holy Spirit
comes upon you, and you will be my witnesses.

Acts 1:8

Due to the fall of mankind, all of us are vulnerable to the misuse of power, as this popular phrase attributed to Lord Acton in the nineteenth century suggests: "Power tends to corrupt. Absolute power corrupts absolutely." In this fallen world, we have good reason to fear the misuse of power, because it is often used to dominate, control, manipulate, abuse, and rebel against legitimate authority. Sadly, our families, workplaces, and church communities can be the environments where we are most wounded by these abuses of power.

Who among us hasn't felt overpowered, controlled, or belittled in some form or fashion? Or perhaps we have experienced the opposite extreme, feeling unprotected or let down by someone failing to act in a particular way, not exercising his proper authority or God-given power. Some of these experiences may even be daily occurrences in our lives. Being on the receiving end of someone's misguided or abusive power can leave us profoundly traumatized, even victimized, for years to come. Experiences like these only accentuate the primordial wound of powerlessness, which is as ancient as sin itself.

Before sin disrupted our unspoiled existence (see Gn 2), Adam and Eve had the power to live as God commanded them. They humbly respected God's ultimate power and lived in holy submission to him. They knew firsthand what all of us must discover, that "strength belongs to God" (Ps 62:12) and that the Almighty exercises his power to love, never to dominate or control. His commands are given to bless and protect, all the while respecting our dignity and freedom. They had no fear of being dominated or abused by him or one another (at least until the deceiver planted seeds of doubt in their minds).

With Adam and Eve's rebellion, however, the misuse of power (sin) and powerlessness (wound) reared their ugly heads. When Eve succumbed to the serpent's temptation, Adam abdicated his role and failed to stand in his proper authority, allowing the evil one dominion over all the earth (see Gn 3, Rom 5:12–14). In choosing to surrender their God-given power and authority over to the eternally powerless one, Adam and Eve also disconnected from the power of the Holy Spirit. As a result, they ended up debilitating themselves and the rest of the human race with the same wound of powerlessness.

After their disobedience, God revealed to Adam that his work, once a source of joy and fulfillment, would become laborious and difficult (due to this curse of powerlessness). God also warned Eve that she would have to contend with the curse of domination by her husband (who would be compensating for his lack of genuine God-given power). She, in turn, out of her powerlessness, would attempt to take over for Adam's ineptness through manipulation and control (see Gn 3:16–19).[1]

—∽—

The apple does not fall far from the tree. Every son and daughter of our first parents has to deal these consequences of powerlessness, domination, and control. We are all prone to the same weaknesses.[2] With our loss of grace, we toil in labor, fear domination, and have a tendency to become passive, controlling, and rebellious, all the while experiencing an inherent weakness in our attempts to resist sin. Though expressed in myriad of ways, this wound of powerlessness is experienced by all.

These human weaknesses and abuses of power have played out throughout history and were on full display during Jesus' crucifixion, when the grotesque evil of worldly power and cowardly powerlessness reached a crescendo. Jesus, on the other hand, gave witness to God's holy power, even while willingly experiencing the powerlessness of having his body nailed to the cross. Continuing to abide with the Father and Holy Spirit in the face of evil, he endured the cross and despised its shame (see Heb 12:1–2). Accepting the curse of our powerlessness and victimization, he made it possible for us to become victors once again (see 2 Cor 2:14).

Rising from the dead, Jesus fully revealed God's mighty power and restored God's dominion on behalf of the human race. Before ascending into heaven, he promised his disciples a share in his resurrection power: "You will *receive power* when the Holy Spirit comes upon you, and you will be my witnesses" (Acts 1:8, emphasis added). This promise was fulfilled on the feast of Pentecost.

Can you envision the disciples in the upper room, praying in unity with Jesus' mother, Mary? As the one person in the room who had previous experience receiving the Holy Spirit, she knew and understood the power of God's Spirit, which brought Jesus into her womb many years earlier. That first time she had to wait nine months. This time she and her spiritual sons only had to wait nine days, intensely praying together until the gift of the Holy Spirit descended upon them. The manifestations of God's mighty power came upon them in the form of a rushing wind, tongues of fire, and the supernatural gift of languages (see Acts 2:1–4). Soon after, the fruit of the Spirit's presence became evident through their love, joy, peace, fortitude, wisdom, understanding, and faithfulness. The disciples were transformed from wounded men and women hiding in a locked room to powerhouses of grace, transforming the world and living and dying as witnesses for Christ.

Confirmed in the power of the Holy Spirit, Peter spoke boldly before the stunned crowds gathered from every nation. He made it abundantly clear that this gift of God's power was available to all people: "Repent and be baptized, every one of you, in the name of Jesus Christ for the forgiveness of your sins; and you will receive the gift of the Holy Spirit. For the promise is made to you and to your children and to all those far off, whomever the Lord our God will call" (Acts 2:38–39).

You and I are counted among those who are far off. All of us who believe in Christ and are baptized are invited to renounce demonic and worldly power and receive God's holy power. According to Church teaching, this grace is given in the sacrament of Confirmation, which is "the special outpouring of the Holy Spirit as once granted to the apostles on the day of Pentecost" (*CCC*, 1302). Isn't that amazing? You and I are invited to receive the same fullness of power that enabled the disciples to heal the sick, raise the dead, and speak out boldly as Christ's courageous witnesses to change the world.

Let's pause here a moment to take this to heart and see how this applies to each of us personally.

Take a Moment

1. What did you experience when you received the Holy Spirit (through the sacrament of Confirmation)? If you haven't been confirmed, describe any experiences you have had with the Holy Spirit.

2. What attachments, relationships, desires, and so forth prevent you from yielding more fully to the Holy Spirit?

3. How does Holy Spirit power differ from demonic worldly power? Give examples of both kinds of power influencing your life.

—⁂—

Considering these questions for myself, I realize that my awareness of the Holy Spirit has changed dramatically since my Confirmation. I received the sacrament at the age of thirteen, but I did not really have any kind of a profound experience or awareness of the Holy Spirit's presence. That would happen twenty years later. Looking back, though, I can see that the Holy Spirit was always working invisibly in my life, giving me the strength to love, hope, believe, and choose the good in many situations in my life. I can also see how various gifts and fruits of the Holy Spirit were operating in my life back then (see 1 Cor 12:4–7, Rom 12:1–6, Is 11:2, Gal 5:22–23). But none of this was obvious to me at the time. Not really appreciative of the gift, I did not actively yield to the Holy Spirit's influence in my daily decision-making.

Ironically, the year I received my Confirmation was when I was most conscious of feeling powerless in my life. That year, everything in my surroundings seemed out of control: my dad left, my basketball coach tried to molest me, and I felt betrayed by my best friends and girlfriend.[3] Left to care for seven children by herself, my mom seemed overwhelmed. Though confirmed in the power of the Holy Spirit, I was not consciously aware that I could actively draw on the strength of the Holy Spirit to help me deal with these difficult circumstances. Instead, I grasped for control the only way I knew how: by disconnecting my heart from those I loved and putting a fortress around it.

I found "power" through ungodly self-reliance and judgments as well as through my striving to do well in sports and school. One regrettable day, I even compensated for my powerlessness by bullying a weaker classmate. All of these, in retrospect, were attempts to prove myself and others that "I have what it takes."[4] Of course, these attempts to feel powerful only served to further conceal my underlying wounds of powerlessness and further strengthen my false self. None of these superficial attempts at power brought genuine healing or the kind of internal strength that only the Holy Spirit is capable of providing for any of us.

My conscious awareness of the Holy Spirit came in my early thirties, when I was invited by a friend to attend a Bible study. While there, one of the men shared some of the powerful manifestations of the Holy Spirit in his life, and I wanted to learn more about this third person of the Trinity. I began studying the scriptures to learn more, and I soon discovered that our parish offered a Life in the Spirit seminar.

During the seminar, I could sense the Holy Spirit cultivating a supernatural desire in me for a greater release of his presence and power in my life. But when it finally came time to receive prayer, I became afraid of losing control, so I closed my heart again in self-protection. Because of my control, I had a difficult time allowing the Holy Spirit to flow freely in and through me. I had not yet dealt with my wounds of powerlessness or begun to face my self-reliance and judgments that kept me in control. I discovered I was much more enthusiastic about learning things about the Holy Spirit than experiencing his manifest presence. Before I could yield to his powerful love, I needed healing of these wounds and repentance for my sin of control.

A few years later, after some necessary healing and yielding of control, I experienced a powerful outpouring of the Holy Spirit during my Christ Renews His Parish retreat.[5] From that point forward, I began to recognize the gifts and fruit of the Holy Spirit in my life and in those around me who were also actively seeking God (see Is 11:2, Rom 12:1–6, 1 Cor 12:4–7, Gal 5:22–23). Through those spiritual gifts, I could discern the difference between the spiritual fruit called "self-control" and my fearful control that came out of my wounds of powerlessness and gave power to demonic strongholds in my life. This awareness gradually changed the way I prayed and related to others. Repenting of control, I yielded more to the Holy Spirit's gentle power. (This is an ongoing journey, of course.) I also developed a greater desire to learn and understand more of what the scriptures and Church taught about God's authentic power.

Through my study of scripture and Church teaching, I realized that events in both the Old and New Testament gave context to the way we practice the sacrament of Confirmation in the Church today. Beginning in the Old Testament, I saw that the Holy Spirit was given exclusively to God's carefully chosen servants, first to the seventy elders called to assist Moses and then to the psalmists and artisans who were commissioned to work in the holy Temple in Jerusalem.

Soon after, priests, prophets, and kings were also "anointed" with the Holy Spirit. In the ceremony of anointing, blessed oil was poured over their heads, and the Holy Spirit came upon them and remained with them (see Ex 29:7, 40:9; 1 Kgs 19:16; 2 Kgs 9:6; Ps 89:21). We get a glimpse of this ritual of consecration when the prophet Samuel anointed David king of Israel: "Then Samuel, with the horn of oil in hand, anointed him in the midst of his brothers, and from that day on, the Spirit of the Lord rushed upon David" (1 Sm 16:13). I love the imagery here: "the Spirit of the Lord *rushed* upon David." Sounds like a gushing waterfall of the Holy Spirit, doesn't it?

These Old Testament passages also provide a context for why Jesus and his disciples used blessed oil to anoint during their ministry. And why blessed oil continues to be used today in the sacraments of Baptism, Confirmation, and Holy Orders, as well as for the Anointing of the Sick. The anointing with oil is an outward symbol of a profound spiritual grace—the inward "anointing with the Holy Spirit."

As I continued studying the prophets of the Old Testament, I began to see that many of them foretold the coming of the Messiah, the one ordained to fulfill the roles of priest, prophet, and king (see Heb 6:20, Acts 3:22–23, Mt 27:11). Like the ordained of old, the Messiah would be anointed by the Spirit to carry out God's work, offering sacrifice for sin (priest), proclaiming the justice and mercy of God (prophet), and ensuring that God's kingdom would reign (king). The following prophecy from Isaiah lays out the Messiah's mission and the anointing, which is essential for accomplishing the mission: "The Spirit of the Lord God is upon me, because the *Lord has anointed me*; he has sent me to bring good news to the afflicted, to bind up the brokenhearted, to proclaim liberty to the captives, release to the prisoner . . . to comfort all who mourn" (Is 61:1–2, emphasis added).

In reflecting on this passage, Mary Healy in her book *Healing* observes, "Jesus chose precisely this passage [Isaiah 61] to define the essence of his mission. His very title Messiah (or in Greek, Christ)

means 'Anointed One' and derives from that anointing at his baptism.
. . . The Isaiah passage also describes the mission itself. The purpose
of Jesus' anointing was so that he could 'proclaim good news to the
poor'—good news that includes not only helpful words but the *very
realities* that the words announce—freedom, healing, and release
from captivity."[6]

After publicly proclaiming this passage in his hometown synagogue, Jesus did what he spoke, as the anointing of the Spirit empowered him to preach a message of great hope, heal those who were
infirmed, and bring liberty to all those bound by sin and evil (see Lk
4:18–19, Acts 10:38). This mission of healing and setting captives
free reached its apex on the cross.

Jesus imparted the anointing of the Spirit to his disciples and promised
the same gift to all of us in every nation who would be called by his
name (see Acts 2:1–13, 38–39; 8:14; 10:44–48; 19:2–7; see also 1
John 2:27). Do you realize that the name "Christian" literally means
"anointed one"? The Spirit of the Lord that remained with Jesus is
also in us and upon us, because the Lord has anointed each one of us
to continue his missionary work on earth.

All of us who have been baptized, confirmed, or ordained are
anointed by the Holy Spirit and commissioned to assume an active
share in Jesus' mission. Fr. Raniero Cantalamessa explains, "Anointing is not an act, but rather a state or mode of being and behaving and,
so to say, a whole style of living."[7] That is a beautiful description of
the sacraments, isn't it? They are not just events but a mode of being
and a "whole style of living." Through them we are united with Jesus
to share in his identity and carry out his mission. We, too, are empowered to bring glad tidings to the lowly, to heal the brokenhearted, to
proclaim liberty to captives, release to the prisoners, and to comfort
all who mourn. This is how we are called to live the grace of Confirmation in our lives. It is not just an event that happened years ago but
a "mode of being" and "whole style of living," today and every day.

This understanding that we all share in Jesus' anointing and mission became much more real to me about twenty years ago when a missionary team from New York City visited our parish in Florida to offer a five-day parish renewal. In preparing for the first night, the presenting team asked me if I would be willing to proclaim Isaiah 61 to start the mission. They requested I speak without a microphone as though I stood in the place of Jesus speaking in the synagogue after his Baptism.

When I stood up, the church was dark, and I began to proclaim boldly: "The Spirit of the Lord is upon me, because the Lord has anointed me." As the words came out of my mouth, I felt the power of the Spirit rush through me and through the words I was speaking. I trust others could feel his presence, too, because the mission team asked me afterward if I would proclaim it again for the next four nights. It turned out to be an amazing experience for me personally (and I hope for others, too). Each time I stood up to proclaim these words from Isaiah 61, the message became more indelibly etched in my mind and heart. I sensed the Holy Spirit telling me, "This is not just Jesus' mission, but yours as well—and every other Christian who has been baptized and confirmed."

Does that include you? If so, I invite you to allow these realities to be indelibly etched in your mind and heart. Allow the name *anointed one* to become part of your fundamental identity. If you have been baptized and confirmed in Christ, the same Holy Spirit who anointed and empowered Jesus dwells in you and acts through you. You are the Father's beloved. Jesus' abiding presence remains with you. You are anointed with the full power of the Holy Spirit. Jesus' mission has become *your mission*. You are anointed to proclaim the Good News, to heal the brokenhearted, to set the captives free, and to comfort all who mourn. You don't need to worry about feeling inadequate—he has given you his own power to overcome your powerlessness.

—〜〜—

The apostle Paul understood these realities and lived them confidently, remarking, "I have the strength for everything through him who empowers me" (Phil 4:13). The same Holy Spirit who enabled Jesus to love so completely gave St. Paul and each one of us the ability to lay down our lives for our friends and to bless our enemies. The power of the Holy Spirit enabled Jesus to heal, perform miracles, and even raise the dead. That same Spirit in St. Paul and in us gives us the capacity to do the same things.

The power that moved Jesus with compassion for the needy and gave him the courage and strength to go to the cross dwells in us and enables us to be compassionate and to take up our cross and follow him. This same Spirit, who kept Jesus free from sin, convicts us when we sin and gives us the capacity to become whole and holy, in union with him. There are no limits to what we are capable of doing because of this anointing power from the Holy Spirit that we have received through the sacraments. We are no longer powerless, as long as we yield to the power of the Holy Spirit in our lives. But, the opposite is also true. Without the Holy Spirit, we can do nothing of any lasting fruit (see Jn 15:5). Because of the fall, we really are powerless to follow Jesus or carry out his mission without his anointing. We all realize this, don't we? On our own we aren't capable of doing any of the things Jesus did. We are not capable of love, miracles, great courage, or any other virtue apart from his "virtue" (this word literally means "strength").

But here's the really good news: we do not need to rely on our own strength when we feel powerless. Jesus encouraged St. Paul with these words when he was struggling with his own incapacities: "For power is made perfect in weakness" (2 Cor 12:9). That is great news, isn't it? We don't have to be strong by ourselves because God is all-powerful. Like St. Paul, we can "boast in our weaknesses." Many of us have a habit of boasting in our human capacities, but this only blocks the power of the Holy Spirit in our lives.

—m—

I can personally attest to how self-reliance blocks the movement of the Holy Spirit. And I have also observed how his anointing flows most freely when we let go of control and become vulnerable. One such occurrence happened in my life during a nine-day fast, when I became very weak and found it difficult to focus. On the eighth day of the fast, I went into work at my counseling office and could barely function. But as the day progressed, one person after another had the biggest healing breakthrough of their lives. I gave very little counsel. I didn't even pray with most of the people. Actually, I didn't do much of anything but sit there depleted of my own strength.

The *anointing* from the Holy Spirit did all the work. God wanted to show me what spiritual poverty looked like so he could demonstrate his power in and through my weaknesses. After it was all over, the only thing I could do was praise him and realize how deluded I had been about my own capabilities. I realized in a whole new way that, despite my many years of training and experience, apart from him I could do nothing (see Jn 15:4).

A similar experience of relying on God in the midst of my powerlessness occurred while teaching a Sexual Healing and Redemption course at the Theology of the Body Institute in Pennsylvania. As the title suggests, the material can be rather intense, dealing with sexual sins, wounds, and identity issues. In the months leading up to the course, our team met over the phone to pray for the participants and to prepare all of our hearts for what we sensed was going to be a very powerful encounter with the risen Lord. Throughout that time, Fr. Mark Toups, our chaplain for the course, kept hearing that we needed to pray for "spiritual poverty" (see Mt 5:3). He encouraged each of us to ask for that grace of docility to the Holy Spirit daily in preparation for the course. We had no idea at the time why this posture of spiritual poverty would prove to be so important.

Once the course began, Fr. Mark and I met privately every morning to pray together and prepare for the day. The theme of spiritual poverty continued to surface in our prayer and discussion together, and this carried over into the teaching. The first few days of the class, I remained docile to the Holy Spirit and the students seemed very receptive and hungry to learn. But as the days progressed, their wounds and sins came bubbling to the surface. Frustration and anger (often symptoms of powerlessness) began to manifest by Tuesday afternoon. By Wednesday morning everyone seemed overwhelmed by the pain they were feeling. (Being overwhelmed is another symptom of powerlessness.) By the time I stood up in front of the class to teach Wednesday afternoon, I could see that many had shut down mentally and emotionally. As I began to lay out the lesson, it was as though I was speaking to a brick wall. The students couldn't receive any more truth or conviction.

Without realizing it, seeing their lack of receptivity and their evident pain, I, too, began to feel powerless and didn't know how to reach them. After a few minutes of seeing their unresponsiveness, I stopped the class to consult with Fr. Mark. Together, we discerned that we were to dismiss the class and encourage everyone to head outside for recreation. That night almost everyone in the class brought their pain and sin to the priests in the sacrament of Reconciliation. Afterward, I could see some lifting of the spirit of oppression that was causing the powerlessness.

The next morning, when I met Fr. Mark for our prayer time together before class, I was still feeling oppressed and powerless. I confessed to him that I had no inspiration for the morning and was reluctant to stand up in front of the class again. After hearing my confession, his advice was priceless, though it was the last thing I wanted to hear: "Great. This is the moment we have been praying about for months—this is your spiritual poverty." I responded with, "That is easy for you to say—I'm the one that has to get up to teach." He retorted, "No you don't; that's up to God. Just stand up there and let him do what he wants."

Feeling extremely vulnerable, I stood up in front of the hundred or so students with nothing to offer. The subject that morning was healing, which is a topic I ordinarily love to discuss. But after asking them to open the workbook to those pages, I felt a check in my spirit and heard the inaudible voice of the Holy Spirit in my thoughts: "Don't teach. Just proclaim Isaiah 61 (the introductory scripture in the notes) and allow Jesus to speak through you." Stepping out in faith, with some trepidation, I yielded to the leading. As soon as I did, the Holy Spirit came upon me with his strong presence, and I boldly proclaimed these words (again without a microphone): "The Spirit of the Lord is upon me, because the Lord has anointed me. He has sent me . . . to heal the brokenhearted, to proclaim liberty to the captives . . . to comfort all who mourn."

What happened next is impossible to adequately describe. But to give you an idea, that class is now dubbed "Pentecost Thursday" by some of the students. None of us could have possibly imagined what was about to take place when these words were proclaimed under the anointing of the Holy Spirit. Before I could finish proclaiming the scripture, people throughout the room began weeping. For many, their sobs quickly turned into wailing. Then just as suddenly as the crying started, it stopped, and a wave of deep peace descended upon everyone. After a time of profound silence, rejoicing began to spread throughout the room, as our "mourning turned into joy" (Jer 31:13). One person began to sing a song of praise to the Lord, and within seconds the whole class joined in spontaneously, worshiping God in unison with heartfelt gratitude.

As a spirit of awe and wonder filled the room, one after another stood up and shared how Jesus personally came to them and healed their broken hearts, released them from their places of captivity, and comforted them in their mourning. While the words of Isaiah 61 were being proclaimed, they said they felt the Holy Spirit rushing upon them and moving through them. The students described experiences of seeing Jesus, hearing him speak very personally to them, and many said he touched them physically and healed them. Others had visions of Jesus ministering to their childhood memories and wounds; many were healed of deep-seated sexual compulsions and the wounds that underlie these habitual sins.

For me, the entire experience was a demonstration of God's power being perfected in our weaknesses (see 2 Cor 12:9). Just as the Beatitude promised, the kingdom of heaven really did descend among us as we stood there helplessly in our spiritual poverty. Later that day,

Fr. Mark and I laughed with the joy of little children. There is nothing I could have taught that could compare with what Jesus did in the hearts of those students. It turned out that Jesus was teaching me the lesson of a lifetime that day, one that I must continually relearn: I had to let go of my control and give the Holy Spirit freedom to do what he desired. Praise be to God, for he is more than capable, especially when we recognize that we are not!

One of the great joys in my life is seeing people receive deep healing and transformation and then seeing their increased freedom to yield to the Holy Spirit. They move from relying upon their human control to allowing God's power to move through them. Their lives and ministries are renewed, and they in turn touch many others. In the past several years, our team at John Paul II Healing Center has ministered to many consecrated religious. In my mind, they are icons of the sacrament of Confirmation because they have fully dedicated their lives to share in Jesus' mission, each with his or her own unique charism.

The ones I have met over the years have been devoted men and women of all ages who have one thing in common: a heart to serve God and his people. But too often their hearts have also been deeply wounded and overlooked. I am always amazed to discover the depths of their unhealed wounds that are hidden behind their habits. Some of these wounds are quite debilitating, including the shame of sexual abuse, severe rejection and abandonment, and many other traumas, leaving a legacy of fear, confusion, and powerlessness. Many had not shared these hurts with anyone except their bridegroom, Jesus, and had grown weary with hopelessness.

What a great privilege it has been for me and our team to be entrusted into their hearts to facilitate Jesus' healing love for them. As these religious have entered into their healing journeys, it has had a profound effect in many of their ministries. With greater freedom in their hearts, they become capable of a deeper surrender to the Holy Spirit, which in turn increases the anointing grace flowing through their charism. For one brother, his healing process has given him a new zeal and enthusiasm in his gift of evangelization. He now sees healing as a central part of bringing others into a vital relationship with Jesus.

For one religious sister, her personal transformation has been multiplied a hundredfold through her gift of speaking to people of all ages. Her words now communicate so much of the Holy Spirit's love and truth that her listeners receive healing as she delivers her message and shares her testimony. For another group of sisters, their personal healing experiences have influenced the way they prepare students for the sacraments. Recently, I was invited to observe two of them offer a Confirmation retreat to about eighty ninth-graders. The Holy Spirit worked powerfully through these sisters in their newfound vulnerability. The students had a great time, but even more importantly, many of them said they encountered the living God for the first time.

The sisters taught them about the reality and power of the Holy Spirit and the beauty of the sacraments. They witnessed to the students about their need for healing, and they engaged the students in fun activities where they laughed a lot and engaged their hearts. Finally, they invited them into group and individual prayer experiences to encounter the risen Jesus. Many of the young people experienced healing of their wounds and most of them came away with an increased capacity to receive an outpouring of the Holy Spirit on the day of Confirmation. Months later, several of those students shared their experience when the Holy Spirit come upon them with power after their local bishop laid hands on them and anointed them with oil at their Confirmations.

Following the retreat with the sisters, I left yearning for their charism to spread throughout the Church, so that every person preparing to receive the sacrament of Confirmation would more fully experience "the same outpouring of the Holy Spirit as once granted to the apostles on the day of Pentecost" (*CCC*, 1302). Come Holy Spirit, let your fire fall! Can you imagine what might happen in our world if the majority of us who have already been baptized and confirmed in the Church would repent of our worldly power, control, and self-reliance and allow the Holy Spirit's power to be more fully perfected in our weakness? In the next chapter, we will explore what this looks like in the sacrament of Holy Orders.

Before turning our attention there, let's take a moment now to ask the Holy Spirit to prepare our hearts for a greater outpouring of his presence. Remember, you are his *anointed*. The following reflections will help you live more fully from this identity.

Take a Moment

1. In what ways do you cling to false power and control in your life? Be specific.

2. In your opinion, what is the difference between the wound of powerlessness and "spiritual poverty"?

3. Describe some experiences in your life where the Holy Spirit worked through your weaknesses and spiritual poverty.

Scripture Meditation

The following passage from Acts 8:9–19 shows how the early Church practiced Confirmation by calling the apostles to lay hands on the baptized to receive the Holy Spirit. It also contrasts the power of the Holy Spirit from demonic and worldly power. I encourage you to read through this passage three times, slowly, to gain the most benefit.

1. Begin by asking the Holy Spirit to guide you as you reflect on the scripture passage.

2. Read the passage slowly the first time for overall understanding, noticing the contrast between the power of the Holy Spirit and that of demonic and secular forces.

3. Read a second time slowly, seeing how the Holy Spirit came upon the people, and listen to a word or phrase that speaks to your heart.

4. Read a third time, very slowly, allowing the Holy Spirit to speak to you personally; then record what you receive in your journal.

Confirmation in the Early Church

"A man named Simon used to practice magic in the city and astounded the people of Samaria, claiming to be someone great. All of them, from the least to the greatest, paid attention to him, saying, 'This man is the "Power of God" that is called "Great."' They paid attention to him because he had astounded them by his magic for a long time, but once they began to believe Philip as he preached the good news about the kingdom of God and the name of Jesus Christ, men and women alike were baptized. Even Simon himself believed and, after being baptized, became devoted to Philip; and when he saw the signs and mighty deeds that were occurring, he was astounded. Now when the apostles in Jerusalem heard that Samaria had accepted the word of God, they sent them Peter and John, who went down and prayed for them, that they might receive the Holy Spirit, for it had not yet fallen upon any of them; they had only been baptized in the name of the Lord Jesus. Then they laid hands on them and they received the Holy Spirit. When Simon saw that the Spirit was conferred by the laying on of the apostles' hands, he offered them money and said, 'Give me this power too, so that anyone upon whom I lay my hands may receive the Holy Spirit'" (Acts 8:9–19).

Let Us Pray

1. Ask the Father for forgiveness for any areas where you have relied on worldly or demonic power to manipulate, control, dominate, or to rebel against authority. (Then resolve to confess these sins in the sacrament of Reconciliation.)

2. Next, renounce all unholy power, control, manipulation, intimida-
   tion, rebellion, occult practices, powerlessness, victimization, and
   sloth: "In the name of Jesus, I renounce unholy power, control,
   manipulation . . ."

3. Ask the Holy Spirit to fill you with his power and to stir up the
   graces of your Baptism and Confirmation. You may pray in your
   own words from your heart or pray out loud the following prayer
   from Fr. George Montague:

Prayer for Release of the Holy Spirit

Lord Jesus, I want to be your servant, your instrument in bringing
faith, hope, and love into the lives of others.[8] For that I need the gifts
of your Holy Spirit, the word gifts and the service gifts. Please show
me what gifts I need, and help me to grow in the ones you have already given me. Let me not think that my natural talents are sufficient
to build your kingdom. Take what you have given me by nature and
transform it by the anointing of your Holy Spirit. May I, like your
mother (in Luke 1:39–56), be moved to praise, to listen to your word,
to share it, and to serve. Amen.

6

THE FATHER'S AUTHORITY

How Holy Orders Heals Wounds of Confusion

As the Father has sent me, so I send you.
John 20:21

Father Knows Best was a popular television show of my earliest memories. Championing traditional values, the show symbolized the American culture in which I was raised in the late 1950s and early 1960s. This excerpt from the book of Sirach highlights the virtues of honor and respect for authority, which were more prominent at the time: "For the Lord sets a father in honor over his children and confirms a mother's authority over her sons. Those who honor their father atone for sins; they store up riches who respect their mother. . . . When they pray, they are heard" (Sir 3:2–5).

During my formative years, these words of wisdom from Sirach matched the world I experienced around me. I was taught to reverence God and honor his ordained authority. Expectations and roles, following this God-given order, remained clear at home, at church, and at school. Certainly not everyone lived these ideals perfectly in the 1950s, but the value of honoring authority remained unquestioned throughout the culture in most environments. Inside and outside the family, neither disrespect nor rebellion was tolerated, meeting with firm discipline whenever the boundaries of honor were violated.

Among the Catholic faithful, the pope, bishops, and priests represented the hierarchy of authority, and thus garnered the highest honor and respect in our communities. We believed and lived from the assumption that "Father" knows best because we understood implicitly those ordained into Christ's priestly ministry derived their fatherhood from the one true Father who is the source of all genuine authority (see Mt 23:9, Rom 13:1–2, Heb 13:17).

For many Catholics during that era, priests were almost too revered. Many put them on a pedestal, which didn't allow us to see that they had their own brokenness. But these priests were for the most part good fathers, nevertheless. With enough priests for many parishes to have two or three in residence, they seemed ever present. Most, in my experience, displayed a genuine authority, with a servant's heart, and interacted regularly with their spiritual children at our Catholic schools, at our parish functions, and occasionally around the dinner table in our homes. Priests were part of the natural rhythm of family and parish life, and we trusted without question that our "Father" knew what was best for us, his spiritual children.

Things changed quickly in the late sixties. By the time the early seventies rolled around, *rebellion* became the byword in our nation, as riots spread throughout the major cities of the United States. Simultaneously, the drug culture and sexual revolution rose up like a raging flood, washing away traditional social mores. Even the Church experienced a time of chaos with all the disordered misinterpretations of the Second Vatican Council. Priests and religious were leaving the Church by the thousands, as the longstanding norms undergirding family, church, and society were rapidly eroding into a sea of *confusion.*

—⁓—

At the height of this social uprising, I entered my teenage years, the time when many young people naturally question authority as a way of forming their own identity. While all the upheaval was going on in the world around me, my secure foundations at home were also crumbling. Dave, my older brother by two years, immersed himself in the drug culture and embraced the sexual revolution without restraint.

Meanwhile, the authority in our family collapsed when we discovered that my dad was drinking heavily and having an affair. He would later leave the family for good. These events and revelations naturally left my personal world in a state of confusion and disorder.

Losing some respect for our older brother and father, my siblings and I no longer adhered to the "father knows best" philosophy of life. The certitude of wise fatherly authority, whether true or false at an earlier time, was now shattered. Skepticism replaced trust not just with our father but in some way with all those in authority. We soon allowed our disrespectful attitudes and behaviors to infiltrate our relationship with our mother. And with all of that, we dishonored God and his commandments, which had been given as a gift to preserve sacred order in our relationships (see Eph 6:2, Sir 3:2–5).

Without realizing it, my reverence toward God and his priesthood also weakened during those years. Though my experiences with priests continued to be largely positive, my heart no longer trusted them (or anyone else) to speak with God's authority. Priests, and the Church they represented, became just another voice in a confusing cacophony of competing voices. I felt compelled to figure life out on my own, without any authority figure to guide me. Though I was still attending church, I no longer felt anchored there, like I had been earlier in my life. No wonder I was in a crisis of faith by the time I reached my late twenties—I didn't know what to believe or what authority I could trust![1] A popular saying at the time was "Don't trust anyone over thirty." Confusion had insidiously settled into my mind and heart and into our culture as well.

Are you familiar with this experience of not trusting authority and feeling like you have to figure things out on your own? In one way or another, it is a shared human experience on this side of Eden. Some of us are more aware of it than others, perhaps, because our individual life circumstances make it more obvious. But all of us are subject to this tendency toward ungodly self-reliance, which is as old as history itself. Ultimately, it is rooted in the serpent's lie in the Garden of Eden suggesting that we can be our own self-appointed authority, knowing what is good and evil, apart from God (see Gn 3).

According to St. John Paul II, our rebellion against God's fatherly authority has permeated all of history since the fall: "*This is truly the key to interpreting reality. . . . Original sin, then, attempts to abolish fatherhood*, destroying its rays . . . placing in doubt the truth about God, who is love."[2] When we doubt the Father's love, wisdom, and integrity, we lose our capacity to trust him and the authority established by him. If left unchecked, we eventually lose touch with the ground of reality itself.

Can you imagine how disorienting it must have been for Adam and Eve to be displaced from their safe haven after their sin? The Father's benevolent authority, once a source of their protection and intimate care, suddenly became threatening to them. Nothing made sense anymore. They were lost in the truest sense of the word. Their rebellion brought chaos and disruption not only to their lives but also to ours. Since that cataclysmic moment, confusion and disorder have been running rampant in our world. The massive rebellion that shook our culture in the 1960s, and in some way permeates our society and families today, is merely a reflection of that original uprising in the garden.

You may ask, as I have, what can heal us collectively and individually from this primordial wound of confusion and disorder? Since the wound is rooted in distorted perceptions of the Father's authority and our rebellion against his authority, the antidote must be the opposite: restoring our understanding of his authority and humbly submitting to that authority in our lives. It makes sense, doesn't it? If confusion is the result of everything being out of order then the restoration of God's plan, putting everything back in its proper place, is what is needed to give us clear vision and understanding of God's holy order.

Who better than the Father's only begotten Son to show us what holy order looks like? This is precisely what Jesus did when he came to earth. He honored his mother and father and obeyed them (see Lk 2:51), he submitted to the proper authorities, and above all else he humbly submitted himself continually to his Father's mission and authority. Through his entire life, death, and resurrection, he only did what the Father showed him and told him to do (see Jn 5:19, 12:49).

Jesus' holy submission to his Father's authority provides a beautiful lesson and model in humility for all of us (see Phil 2:5–9). Unlike Adam, who rebelled against God's authority and submitted to the father of lies, Jesus never ceased trusting in his Father's goodness and guidance, even when the father of lies tried to deceive him (see Mt 4:1). Jesus did not set out to blaze his own path but willingly submitted to the Father's ordained way in all things. Ultimately, the Father granted full authority to Jesus, restoring to mankind the dominion that was lost when Adam disobeyed (see Mt 28:18).

What about the rest of us? How well do we submit ourselves to the Father and to the authority he has established through Jesus? If we are honest, we all fall short in this area. It took me awhile to acknowledge my sin in this realm of submitting to authority. Watching my brother's rebellion, I was less inclined to follow suit. I thought I was the obedient son, submitting to authority. But in reality, my heart did not rest in true submission to the Father. I was more like the older brother in the prodigal son story, staying home and doing all the right things but not really trusting the Father's love.

During a season of intense healing and conversion, the Holy Spirit revealed to me that my confusion came from my lack of trust in authority, and ultimately, this pointed back to my lack of trust in the Father himself. He further showed me through the mirror of scripture that I had covered this wound with an attitude of *insolence* with regard to authority. At first I resisted this revelation, not even understanding the meaning of the word "insolence." Once I learned that it meant arrogance or haughtiness, I certainly didn't want to see myself in that way. After all, I didn't outwardly disrespect authority or rebel against it; I just quietly relied on myself. I had almost imperceptibly become my own authority. I didn't realize that my self-reliance was actually insolence in disguise.

But inwardly, through my lack of trust, I acted as though I was wiser than all the authority around me, including the Church. A prime example came when I read and studied the scriptures. I trusted my own personal interpretations more than the Church's teaching authority. I preferred my own reasoning capacity over the Church's two-thousand-year track record of being guided by the Holy Spirit. But isn't it funny how God works to show us our folly?

During that season, I was inspired to study some of the earliest writings in the Church, starting with St. Ignatius of Antioch in the first century AD. Discovering what he had to say about authority shocked me out of my insolence and led me to question my self-sufficiency. In several of his letters written to the churches in Southeast Asia, he referred to the bishop as the living image of God the Father.[3] He went on to warn that anyone who does not lovingly submit to the bishop's authority rebels against the Father himself.

When I first read these words I was perplexed and wondered how this could be. It almost seemed blasphemous to me, putting a human being in the place of God. But what it really revealed is that I didn't understand the sacrament of Holy Orders. In praying about this, I was led to pray and study the scriptures and Church history, to see if this teaching was from God or merely from human origins. What I discovered led me to totally rethink my stance in relation to authority, which in turn began to heal longstanding wounds of confusion that had plagued me since my teenage years.

Asking for the Holy Spirit's guidance, I began searching the New Testament and almost immediately came across this verse: "Let every person be subordinate to the higher authorities, for *there is no authority except from God*, and those that exist have been *established by God*. Therefore, whoever resists authority opposes what God has appointed, and those who oppose it will bring judgment on themselves" (Rom 13:1–2, emphasis added).

As I read these words, I shuddered, wondering how much judgment I had brought upon myself over the years. But I also rationalized that these words were only referring to governing authority in society and not authority in the Church. My relief was short-lived. I would soon be corrected, once again.

As I continued my study, I began to see how authority was passed down from the Father to Jesus to the apostles as a way of perpetuating his sacramental presence in the world (see Jn 20:21–22, Mt 18:20). Over time, these men passed Jesus' sacred authority onto other men, through the Holy Spirit. They became spiritual fathers for their communities. This, I soon discovered, represented the earliest expression of the sacrament of Holy Orders (see 2 Tm 1:6, 1 Tm 3:1, Tt 1:5, and Acts 6:1–6).

—m—

Finally, I could see the link to St. Ignatius's words and the necessity of my obedience to the authority that God appointed in the letter to the Hebrews: "Obey your leaders and defer to them, for they keep watch over you and will have to give an account" (13:17). When I eventually turned to the *Catechism*, the links became even clearer: "Holy Orders is the sacrament through which the mission entrusted by Christ to his apostles continues to be exercised in the Church until the end of time: thus it is the sacrament of apostolic ministry" (*CCC*, 1536). Since the earliest days of the Church, the Father's holy authority has been passed down through all the generations. This authority of bishop, priest, and deacon has existed in some form throughout the centuries to preserve unity in Christ's body, to protect the members from error and deception, and most importantly, to keep the faithful under the protective care of the Father's wise and benevolent authority.

Do you see how the sacrament of Holy Orders is God's healing remedy to correct the unholy disorder that came into the world with original sin? Through this sacrament, the Father, who is the author of all things, reestablishes his authority through those who bear his image, so "that the people of God abide in the truth that liberates" (*CCC*, 890). This authority is not just for certain groups in the Church but for the entire Body of Christ. And it is not just for the Church; it is intended by God for the healing of the entire world (see *CCC*, 775).

Where original sin attempted to abolish God's fatherhood on earth through Adam's rebellion, this gift of God's fatherly authority in Christ (Holy Orders) seeks to restore it for everyone. It is the bond that holds God's family together, reestablishing his Trinitarian order where chaos and ungodly control have reigned in the world. Every single one of us is called to be a priest of Christ, each according to his or her respective calling. The ministerial priesthood serves the common priesthood of all believers (see *CCC*, 1547). Furthermore, those ordained by Jesus are commissioned to see that every person in heaven and on earth learn to freely "bow their knees before the Father" so that all can discover their true identity in Christ (see Eph 3:16).

There's a lot here for us to assimilate, so let's take a moment to apply these understandings to each of our lives personally.

Take a Moment

1. How does the wound of confusion and disorder manifest in your life? How does it affect the way you relate to authority?

2. What is your reaction to St. Ignatius's saying: "He who submits to the bishop submits to God the Father"?

3. When you think about submitting to authority, what are your emotional reactions? Is submission desirable or frightening for you? Why?

—ɯ—

Does it makes sense that your identity only becomes clear when you submit yourself to our heavenly Father? The Father is the only one capable of telling any of us who we truly are because he alone fully knows our hearts and purpose in life. If we don't trust him and submit to him, doing all he tells us to do, how can we possibly become the unique person he created us to be? St. James conveys this truth with a bit of humor: "Be doers of the word and not hearers only, deluding yourselves. For if anyone is a hearer of the word and not a doer, he is like a man who looks at his own face in a mirror. He sees himself, then goes off and promptly forgets what he looks like" (Jas 1:22–24).

Have you ever left a mirror and forgot what you look like? James is using the physical analogy to speak to a spiritual reality. Spiritually, to forget what we look like is to lose our sense of identity as beloved sons and daughters of the Father. Remember Jesus is that mirror that shows us who we are, and his image continues on the earth through the sacrament of Holy Orders. The Father gives the gift of ordination to those called to represent him so that all may be transformed in Christ. Through this grace of Holy Orders, the Father's authority is restored in our world, in the Church, and in each of our personal lives.

But you may wonder, as I have, how sin-infected and wounded human beings can reveal the face of Christ to us. And how can they represent the Father's heart to the rest of the world? We certainly all know of bishops, priests, deacons, and even popes throughout history who have not represented Jesus well. But that does not take away from their calling and anointing to be his representatives in a way that is different from how the rest of us are called to reflect his image. Obviously no human being can represent Christ perfectly, but the Holy Spirit works through each of us in our weaknesses (see 2 Cor 12:8–10). Since Jesus himself gave this authority and promised his presence (see Mt 16, 18, 28), it is his authority, working through human weakness, which is the basis of our trust. "Since it is ultimately Christ who acts and effects salvation through the ordained minister, the unworthiness of the latter does not prevent Christ from acting. St. Augustine states this forcefully: 'As for the proud minister, he is to be ranked with the devil. Christ's gift is not thereby profaned: what flows through him keeps its purity . . . and if it should pass through defiled beings, it is not itself defiled'" (*CCC*, 1584).

The lack of wholeness or holiness of ordained ministers does not stop the graces of God from flowing through them. Jesus still acts through his ministers in the sacraments for the benefit of those who receive them. However, that does not imply that the holiness or wholeness of the minister is unimportant. In fact, it is vitally important to the effectiveness of their mission and witness in Christ. In order to effectively represent Christ, all ministers of the gospel, including every bishop, priest, and deacon, must grow into their true identity as sons of the Father and as representatives of his fatherhood in the world. For this to happen, their own hearts must be submitted to the Father's authority. This is why the personal healing and transformation of those who have been ordained is not optional. It is essential.

As I mentioned in chapter 4, one of the great joys in our ministry at John Paul II Healing Center is walking with seminarians, deacons, priests, and bishops in their personal journey of healing and transformation. We are merely playing a small part in fulfilling St. John Paul II's vision (which is ultimately Jesus' own vision) for helping them grow into their true identity. As they learn how to become beloved sons, they can become ever more faithful fathers, bringing this restoration to their spiritual children.[4]

Recently I had a conversation about these issues of authority and submission with a priest I have come to know and love over the past several years. During the time I have known Fr. Joseph,[5] he has been on a fast track of healing, restoring his identity as a beloved son and faithful father. Acknowledging that he was particularly wounded in his relationship with his earthly father, he now sees how these wounds have influenced his relationship with his heavenly Father and created much confusion and disorder in his life. His wounds have made it particularly difficult for him to freely submit to the Father and his appointed authority figures. Lacking a healthy attachment with his father and feeling unloved by him growing up has made it more difficult for Fr. Joseph to submit to those in authority in his spiritual family. As a priest, these issues have created a particular dilemma in his life because holy submission is the fundamental call of the priesthood, to be yielded sons of the Father, like Jesus.

As a seminarian, Fr. Joseph was required to submit to the leaders in his seminary and to those in authority over him in his religious order. On the day he received the sacrament of Holy Orders, he prostrated himself in front of the altar as a sign of his complete submission to the Father and as a living sacrifice to Jesus. Later in the ceremony, he knelt before his bishop, clasped his hands, and verbally pledged to this spiritual father (and his successors) that he would be a faithful son. I have no doubt he made his sacred vows with complete sincerity and with a humble heart, as best he could.

These steps of surrendering his will to the Father's will and submitting himself under authority have been instrumental in his healing process. He has purposed to live these vows with a good heart. And those in authority over him have taken great pains in guiding and leading him to be the best priest he can possibly be. Like all good priests, Fr. Joseph loves Jesus and recognizes that his life is crucified and raised with Christ. Jesus lives and moves through him, as he does through all priests, to turn bread and wine into Christ's body and blood, to forgive sins, and to teach and preach the truth. He does all these supernatural functions as a priest, and many more. And he does them with love for his spiritual children and for his Lord.

But here's the rub: though Fr. Joseph has grown in his outward submission to authority, there remain places of his attitudes that are locked in adolescent rebellion against his father. Though he submits outwardly to authority, his heart is not fully submitted, which in turn causes him considerable anxiety and confusion. In those unsettled places of his heart, he does not really trust the Father or his superiors to have his best interest in mind. He is constantly trying to figure out a new angle to avoid having to trust. This results in much inner turmoil as confusion interferes with his clear thinking.

This is how Fr. Joseph describes his wounds that contribute to his confusion:

> From early childhood I wrongly believed that I was not the beloved son and that I would never achieve success or be good enough. I didn't believe I was lovable. I felt abandoned and rejected by my father, and this in turn exacerbated my fear and shame. Later I resented any situation that resembled these early childhood experiences of abandonment and rejection. I projected all this pain onto my authority figures, defensively resenting them for placing any expectations on me that I was afraid I couldn't meet. I didn't trust they had my self-interest in mind. I was constantly tempted to angry defiance and knew I couldn't do that. So I internally dismissed their authority and judged, rejected, and condemned them as my authority figures.

The above describes Fr. Joseph before his intense season of healing. In the past few years, the Holy Spirit has led him to face these issues, first in the confessional and then in healing prayer, to bring his heart in line with his outward obedience. With the help of some trusted spiritual directors, counselors, and prayer ministers, he has honestly confronted the ways he rebelled inwardly and outwardly in his life, particularly with his father and other authority figures.

In doing so, he has come face to face with his hurt and confusion, while unmasking the identity lies he has believed about himself, first as a son growing up and now as a father in the priesthood. As these lies are confronted by Jesus' truth and love, Fr. Joseph is overcoming confusion over his identity and growing stronger in his true identity as a beloved son, knowing that he is anointed by the Holy Spirit and ordained as a holy priest of Jesus Christ. In union with Jesus, he is learning to be an obedient son and reveal the love of the Father more and more in his ministry.

—ɯ—

In the midst of facing his wounds in relationship with authority, the Holy Spirit revealed to Fr. Joseph that Jesus was also hurt by earthly authority figures (e.g., Herod, Pontius Pilate), but he did not allow these people to define his identity. Instead Jesus continued seeking his identity from the Father and never gave in to confusion or identity lies. He trusted the Father throughout these trials.

These insights have greatly aided Fr. Joseph in his healing process. He is growing in trust and learning to maintain a clear sense of who he is in the Father's eyes, even when things don't go the way he expects them to go with his human authority figures. Just recently he had a situation with his direct authority, which in the past would have hurt him deeply and spurred much confusion and hidden rebellion. This time, he handled it with grace. He now sees that when he remains rooted and grounded in the Son, he can continue to trust the Father and receive his identity from him, no matter what anyone else is doing. He is teaching these same things to his spiritual children. Of course, this is a continual learning process for Fr. Joseph, as it is for all of us.

I admire Fr. Joseph and all the ordained who are dedicated to living authentically as beloved sons and faithful fathers. As we all know, it makes a huge difference in their ministry and in all of our lives as a result. All the children in the family know when a father is safe and loving. This is true in spiritual families as well. To that end, I am reminded of a time when I was preparing to speak to a group of seminarians, and one of our intercessors made this request: "Please tell those seminarians to invest themselves completely in their healing and transformation now because, when they become priests, we need them to be good fathers whom we can trust with our hearts." The seminarians were grateful for this woman's words of encouragement.

I believe most of us would agree that every priest's (and minister's) personal transformation is crucial to his ministry. How can the one we call "father" reveal the Father's love and authority unless he has learned to personally trust him? And how can the heart of the Father be revealed unless those ordained are living in a vital relationship with the Father themselves, as beloved sons in holy submission to his wise authority? Fatherly authority and childlike submission result in God's holy order.

—ɷ—

Forming the identity of holy and whole priests is the goal of the Program of Priestly Formation. Established by the United States Conference of Catholic Bishops, in communion with bishops throughout the world, this blueprint for formation affirms the central importance of the priest's personal integration in four areas of his life—human, spiritual, intellectual, and pastoral—so that his identity may be fully configured to Christ. "The life of priests in the Spirit means their continuous transformation and conversion of heart centered on the integration or linking of their *identity* . . . with their *ministry*."[6]

Can you see why the priest must first be transformed in HIM (Christ's healing, identity, and mission) so that he can bring others into union with Christ in the same way? This need for every priest's sanctification and transformation of identity is expressed with poetic beauty by St. Gregory of Nazianzus in this address to his brother priests:

> We must begin by purifying ourselves before purifying others; we must be instructed to be able to instruct, become light to illuminate, draw close to God to bring him close to others, be sanctified to sanctify. . . . I know whose ministers we are, where we find ourselves and to where we strive. I know God's greatness and man's weakness, but also his potential. [Who then is the priest? He is] the defender of truth, who stands with angels, gives glory to archangels, causes sacrifices to rise to the altar on high, shares Christ's priesthood, refashions creation, restores it in God's image, recreates it for the world on high, and even greater, is divinized and divinizes.[7]

Would you agree that St. Gregory knew his identity as a son of the Father and priest of Jesus Christ? He also understood the purpose of Holy Orders:

- to share Christ's priesthood,
- to refashion creation, restoring it in God's image,
- to re-create this world for the kingdom of heaven, and
- to divinize everyone and everything on earth.

Wow. I don't know about you, but those few descriptions leave me in awe at the majesty of God in entrusting Christ's ministry to mortal men.

The God and Father of all creation has chosen a few among us to transform the rest of us into "a kingdom of priests" to worship and serve him for all eternity (see 1 Pt 2:9). When all of us in God's family in heaven and on earth bow our knees before the Father, fully submitting to his authority, there will be no more confusion because we will know who we are in Christ, and all things will be put in their proper and holy order (see Eph 3:14, Rom 14:11).

Let's take a moment now to apply all of this to each of us personally.

Take a Moment

1. What is the difference between the ordained priesthood and the priesthood of all baptized believers? What is the role of each?

2. Why is submission to authority essential in restoring God's holy order in the Church, family, and all of society?

3. Why do you think the ordained first need to heal their identity as beloved sons before becoming faithful fathers? How does Fr. Joseph's history and healing illustrate this process of transformation?

—⁓—

Scripture Meditation

The following passage from John 17 is often referred to as Jesus' High Priestly Prayer. In it, he prays for those he has ordained to carry on his ministry (ministerial priesthood) and then for all believers (common priesthood). I encourage you to reflect on this passage prayerfully, asking the Holy Spirit to reveal what he desires you to receive. For greatest benefit, I suggest you read this three times slowly and reflect on it deliberately.

1. When you read it the first time, pay attention to how Jesus' relationship with the Father influences his relationship with those he consecrates to carry on his work of redemption.

2. On the second time through, read even more slowly and focus on how unity, authority, and consecration in truth are mutually interdependent. Describe why unity and consecration depend on clear authority.

3. Then, for the third time, read it very slowly, asking the Holy Spirit to speak what he desires for you to receive personally from this passage and then record it in your journal.

Jesus' High Priestly Prayer

"Jesus . . . raised his eyes to heaven and said, 'Father, the hour has come. Give glory to your son, so that your son may glorify you, just as you gave him authority over all people, so that he may give eternal life to all you gave him. . . .

[Prayer for Apostles] "'Consecrate them in the truth. Your word is truth. As you sent me into the world, so I sent them into the world. And I consecrate myself for them, so that they also may be consecrated in truth.

[Prayer for All Believers] "'I pray not only for them, but also for those who will believe in me through their word, so that they may all be one, as you, Father, are in me and I in you, that they also may be in us, that the world may believe that you sent me. And I have given them the glory you gave me, so that they may be one, as we are one, I in them and you in me, that they may be brought to perfection as one, that the world may know that you sent me and that you loved them even as you loved me. Father, they are your gift to me'" (Jn 17:1–2, 17–19, 20–24).

Let Us Pray

The following prayer addresses issues of authority and our proper submission to all that God has ordered for our good. This composite prayer encompasses many different types of prayer, including praise, thanksgiving, repentance, forgiveness, healing, renouncing, and surrender.

Prayer Regarding Relationships with Authority

Heavenly Father, I praise your greatness, acknowledging that all authority in heaven and on earth belongs to you. Thank you for sharing your authority with Jesus and to those he entrusted with perpetuating his ministry in the Church so that we may know you and live according to your plan and purpose.

I am sorry for the ways I have rebelled against or disregarded your direct authority, including those you have appointed to guide, teach, and protect me. Please forgive me for my arrogance and insolence in any ways I have thought or acted like I know better than the authority you appointed. Please help me to continually grow in submission to your will as your Holy Spirit leads me.

I forgive all those in authority who have misrepresented you in any way (name specific ones here), and I ask you to heal me from the wounds of confusion and mistrust that have been caused because of that misrepresentation. Father, please bless those in authority who have distorted your image in my eyes, and teach them how to be true sons and fathers in communion with Jesus (pray specifically for each one, prayers to bless them where they have hurt you).

Father you alone know who I am, my dignity, and my calling. I renounce any misdirected authority I have given to anyone else to tell me who I am, what my worth is, or what my calling is. I now place that trust and authority in you, Father, and ask you to speak through your appointed authority in my life to bless and affirm my identity and calling. Thank you.

I now surrender myself to you and to the authority you have appointed. I promise, with your help, to continue to submit myself to you and to your appointed authority so that I can live according to your holy will. I pray all this in the name and holy authority of the Father, Son, and Holy Spirit. Amen.

7

GOD'S
FAITHFUL LOVE

How Holy Matrimony Heals Wounds of Fear

What God has joined together,
no human being must separate.

Matthew 19:6

Despite the well-known fact that marriage is poorly regarded in modern society (as evidenced by high divorce rates and recent trends in cohabiting and premarital sex), God intended the sacrament of Matrimony to be the source of love and life in every family and the foundation of security for every human person. As St. John Paul II has so eloquently stated, the family is the center and the heart of the civilization of love and the first school of love.[1] Every child's heart and overall well-being is formed in this school of love between his or her parents. When bonds of love are secure, children and adults alike experience a pervasive sense of peace and joy, which allows them to thrive and develop to their fullest potential. Having their identity rooted and grounded in God's faithful love (see Eph 3:16), these secure love bonds enable all the members of the family to experience peace, freedom, and a nourishing intimacy.[2]

The converse is also true. The absence of God's faithful love in marriage and family life leaves everyone feeling insecure. Children and spouses are then schooled in the way of fear and eventually form what researchers call "fear bonds."[3] These pseudo-bonds formed in the absence of love are fortified by proud judgments and confining self-protections. In this kind of environment it is difficult for married couples and children alike to find genuine connectedness or develop lasting trust with one another. These wounds of fear instinctively motivate all the members of the family to remain isolated in order to avoid more pain, thus creating environments rife with mistrust, which in turn increases fear and mistrust.

This problem goes all the way back to the fall of mankind, when Adam and Eve broke their covenant with God and subsequently invited seeds of division, mistrust, and infidelity into all human relationships (see Gn 3). Since then, every relationship that is not formed and sustained by God's Spirit eventually becomes unfaithful to one degree or another. This is most damaging in marriage because God intended the marital covenant to be the place where his faithful love would be on display for all to see and experience.

The faces of unfaithfulness are many. Divorce and adultery represent major breaches in marital fidelity, but they are not the only ones. Belittling one's spouse or family members with words or actions is a form of unfaithfulness. Withholding love is unfaithfulness. Judging one another is unfaithfulness. Looking at pornography is unfaithfulness. Holding grudges and failing to forgive is unfaithfulness. Gossiping about one's spouse to friends and relatives is unfaithfulness. None of these infidelities, no matter how large or small, allows Jesus' love to permeate the marriage relationship. Instead, they serve to spread fear and mistrust, permeating through the family like a deadly cancer.

As spouses and children internalize these hurtful interactions, a pervasive sense of insecurity settles into each of their souls, leaving wounds that could last a lifetime if not healed. Moreover, when the bonds of love between a husband and wife are completely broken, their own hearts and the hearts of their children likewise become violently ripped apart in the process (see Mal 2:16). At times like this, when the bond of love is torn asunder, fear and mistrust often become strongholds in each person's heart.

Among the gravest of consequences of broken relationships is that individual family members internalize a distorted perception of

God, of themselves, and of all human relationships. As a result they lose touch with their true identity. Eventually marriage is devalued and relationships become transitory. Under these conditions, the secure love God intended for every human person seems unreachable, and thus we witness the destructive patterns of relationships that are rampant in our culture.

—ᗯᗯ—

These realities of broken relationships and broken trust were driven home to me many years ago when I was teaching a marriage class at a local community college. It was difficult teaching these ideas about the sacrament of Matrimony in a secular environment where God could not be mentioned and many of the students did not have an experience of a healthy marriage or stable family. So I invited the students to search out the truth on their own and present what they discovered in class debates. Everyone in the class was required to research a topic and sign up for a debate. This one particular class stands out in my memory because it involved a debate about marriage and cohabitation. A young man signed up to present the case for marriage, and a young woman presented the case for cohabitation.

During the debate, many ideas were presented back and forth with increasing intensity, but the closing words from the young woman remain emblazoned in my memory. Feeling as though she was losing the debate by the weakness of her arguments, she blurted out in exasperation, "I don't care what you say. I will never marry and put my children through what I experienced watching my parents each divorce three times." The other students gasped, realizing that this was no longer a debate about ideals, but the revelation of this young woman's broken heart.

Identifying with her pain, I also saw that her resolution was in actuality no solution at all but an unconscious choice she made out of her deep wounds of fear and mistrust.[4] She thought she could protect her heart from allowing it to be broken again and at the same time save her children from the same fate that she experienced growing up in a broken home. But in reality she was tragically insulating herself from her pain and ensuring that it would be passed down to her children, inevitably forming their identities as a mirror of her own brokenness. To raise children and never marry would only reinforce the likelihood of her children becoming fearful and insecure and having difficulties making commitments, treading the same path forged by her parents and perhaps the preceding generations.

After class I approached the young woman to express my compassion for her, letting her know I understood a little bit of the pain of her broken heart from my own experience. But when I tried to help her see the danger of her fearful resolution not to marry and how that might further wound her and her children, she could not see what the other students saw clearly. Fear and mistrust, and her self-protective strategies, kept her from hearing the folly of her resolve.

This experience and many others like it have allowed me to have even more compassion for the millions of people who choose not to trust God's will in their intimate relationships. Many are suffering in similar ways as this young woman. You have probably heard the saying "Hurt [unhealed] people, hurt people." This is a sobering reality. Wounds of fear and mistrust beget even more fear and mistrust, unless God's love intervenes somewhere in the process to restore security and faithfulness.

I continue to hold out hope for this young woman and many others like her because I know from personal experience that Jesus is capable of breaking through these strongholds. When I am tempted to impatience with others, the Father gently reminds me that it is taking me a lifetime to allow him to work in and through my life to restore my trust as well as my capacity to love.

—m—

It took me a while to realize how much I resembled the young woman from my class. I knew I identified with her pain, but I wasn't aware how much my self-protection and self-sufficiency resembled hers.

Like her, I made internal "vows" to protect my heart when I was fourteen years old, after my parents divorced. She resolved to never marry so that she and her children would not go through that pain again. I unconsciously vowed that I would never divorce, for the same reasons. Though my "vows" seemed directly opposite to hers, we each reacted out of wounds of fear and mistrust. Deceived by the father of lies, we both believed that our "vows" (inner resolutions made out of fear) were good for us and the people we would eventually love and hope to protect from being hurt as we had been.

In my deceived mind, my fearful resolution to "never divorce like my parents" seemed similar to my marriage vows, but in reality they came from a completely antithetical spirit. I professed my marriage vows publicly through the power of the Holy Spirit. My fearful inner vows remained unspoken and hidden in darkness. My heart inwardly resolved something like this: "I will never be like my dad and divorce my wife and hurt my children." It took me many years to realize this ungodly resolution originated from my wounds of fear and the judgments that I formed to protect against the hurt. This was hardly the inspiration of the Holy Spirit.

Later, when I married my wife, Margie, I embraced the sacrament of Matrimony and expressed my sacred vows to her with the full intention of loving her for life. But lurking underneath the surface, my fear-motivated vows were hidden in darkness and would later almost destroy our marriage. This realization came to me when I turned thirty-three years old (the age my parents were when they separated). I found myself shut down emotionally, "not in love," and terrified that our marriage would end in divorce, just like my parents'. I was living my worst nightmare, terrified that I would hurt my wife and children the way I had been hurt.

I remain deeply grateful for God's intervention during that most difficult year of my life (and our life together). In saving our marriage, he also preserved each one of us from the devastation of continuing the cycle of broken hearts and broken relationships.[5] During that year, the Holy Spirit began to show me that, like Adam and Eve after the fall, I was projecting my fear onto Margie and blaming her for the ways I was not fulfilled. He also revealed the gaping wounds of fear and mistrust that were buried beneath my judgments and fearful vows.

Looking back, I now appreciate how the graces from the sacrament of Matrimony held us together through that difficult season. When we first spoke our vows to each other on our wedding day, we called on the power of the Holy Spirit in the presence of the Church and all of our family and friends. We solemnly promised "to love, honor, and cherish" each other, "in good times and bad, in sickness and health, for richer or poorer, until death do we part."

As we spoke those sacred vows, we solemnly promised that no matter what the other person did or didn't do, we would remain faithful to God and to one another. We later sealed and consummated these sacred vows that night when we gave ourselves intimately to each other—body, soul, and spirit—becoming "one flesh" (see *CCC*, 1643). This was no casual contract; it was a lifelong covenant that we freely chose to enter into. We understood these vows were indissoluble. As such they called for the total gift of ourselves to one another: "The intimate union of marriage, as a mutual giving of two persons, and the good of the children, demand total fidelity from the spouses and require an unbreakable union between them" (*CCC*, 1646).

Throughout these forty years of our marriage, Margie and I have experienced many ups and downs, reflecting the vicissitudes of life we anticipated in our wedding vows. We have certainly been through good and bad times; we have experienced both sickness and health; we have been poor and had abundance. We have also tasted the insecurity of thinking our marriage wouldn't last as well as the security (for us and our children) of knowing that our marriage is a sacred covenant that will last until death.

From all of these varied experiences, we have discovered a little bit more about God's faithful love toward us in all the fearful and faithless moments of our lives. Even when we are unfaithful, he has promised to remain faithful (see 2 Tm 2:13). This, I believe, is a primary way that our wounds of fear and mistrust are healed. His perfect love casts out all fear (see 1 Jn 4:18), enabling us to give ourselves more freely and fully to one another through the Holy Spirit working through our sacrament.

Can you see how drastically the sacrament of Matrimony differs from the myriad ways of forming and breaking relationships in the world? Only the sacrament, lived in the power of the Holy Spirit, can heal our wounds of fear. All the other worldly sexual relationships are nothing more than disguised infidelities, which in the long run only serve to exacerbate our wounds of fear and mistrust. Unfaithfulness can never heal fearfulness. Only faithfulness can do that. Let's pause here for a moment and reflect on all that has been discussed.

Take a Moment

1. How does the sacrament of Matrimony heal the wounds of fear? Why do you think disordered relationships eventually create only more fear bonds?

2. When have you experienced a broken heart through a broken relationship? Can you identify any judgments or fearful vows you made to protect your heart from further pain?

3. Describe how marriage vows differ from those fearful vows.

After coming through our marital crisis and seeing how my spiritual blindness and selfish attitudes had almost destroyed our marriage, I developed a greater hunger for God's perspective on love and relationships. As I read the scriptures and studied Church teaching, my desire to live God's will in our marriage grew even stronger. But soon I discovered how challenging this could be. One verse from Ephesians struck me as particularly challenging: "Husbands, love your wives, even as Christ loved the Church and handed himself over for her" (Eph 5:25). As I read this verse, I experienced fear and helplessness again and asked myself and God, "How can I possibly love Margie with Christ's love? And what will happen to my needs if I lay my life down for her?"

These are still ongoing questions in my life, but I am realizing more and more that Jesus' self-giving love is not opposed to our personal happiness and fulfillment but in actuality the true path to attaining it. In the same passage from Ephesians, St. Paul adds, "He who loves his wife loves himself" (Eph 5:28). I am slowly (sometimes very slowly) realizing the truth of these words, that when I love Margie, I am actually ensuring not only my own fulfillment but also hers and our children's (and grandchildren's) because we are allowing God's presence to heal our wounds and restore our trust. Only genuine trust, in turn, can bring greater unity and intimacy in our marriage and family life. This kind of self-giving love is the only way that genuine fidelity and trust can grow and last.

Over the years these insights from scripture and Church teaching on the sacrament of Matrimony have been a source of inspiration and instruction for me as a husband, father, and grandfather. Additionally, they have been an invaluable source of wisdom during those years when I served as a marriage and family therapist and taught courses on marriage and sexuality. Today these insights form the core teaching of our *Unveiled* marriage conferences at the John Paul II Healing Center.

On the first night of this conference, we demonstrate a vision of what marriage was like before original sin introduced division and insecurity. We invite three people to stand in for the Trinity, representing Father, Son, and Holy Spirit. Then a married couple volunteers to represent Adam and Eve. We depict them surrounded by the love of the Trinity to show how God intended the marriage relationship to be before sin marred it. Then we show how fear and mistrust enter into the marriage when the couple separates from God. Later in the evening, we show through a reenactment of the wedding ceremony how the sacrament of Matrimony restores this divine intimacy in marriage.

On the second day, we introduce the communication skills that are necessary for building unity and intimacy in marriage, and the five areas of communion that are essential for building trust (and overcoming fear). These five areas are listed in the table below spiritual unity, emotional intimacy, companionship, teamwork, and sexual intimacy. Notice from the table how the five areas of communion each have corresponding communication activities that are critical for developing unity.[6]

Areas of Communion	Means of Communicating
Spiritual unity	Praying and worshipping
Emotional intimacy	Listening and expressing
Companionship	Working and recreating
Teamwork	Submitting and decision-making
Sexual intimacy	Expressing affection and lovemaking

These five areas of communion in marriage build naturally one upon another, like floors of a five-story house. Every house must have a firm foundation. In the sacrament of Matrimony, Jesus is that rock-solid foundation (see Mt 7:24–27). He is God's faithful love and the source of true spiritual unity. Getting married in the Church is the first step in cultivating this foundation, but it is certainly not enough. We must learn to live the sacrament of Matrimony daily. This requires ongoing participation in all the sacraments, along with God's Word and prayer. Together these lead us to a deeper love of God and one another. As the old saying goes, "A family that prays together stays together," because prayer is a continual invitation for God to be the bond that holds the marriage together. In addition, worship integrates us and brings everything else in our lives into right order (see *CCC*, 2114).

With this solid foundation of spiritual communion in place, couples are much more likely to open up to one another and share their thoughts, feelings, and desires. This sharing in turn allows them to cultivate emotional intimacy. Some have referred to emotional intimacy as "into-me-see." The word intimacy literally means "into fear" and requires letting go of our self-protections, taking off our masks, and creating a safe environment for real conversations to occur. When we fail in this regard and hurt each other, as all of us do, trust can be repaired by humbly apologizing and forgiving one another.

When couples are emotionally and spiritually bonded in this way, and have not let resentments build up between them, they naturally desire companionship. They enjoy spending time with each other, whether working, playing, or just relaxing together at the end of the day. When it comes time for planning or making decisions, they are able to develop teamwork. Rather than try to control or manipulate each other to get what they selfishly want, they are able instead to look out for each other's interests (see Phil 2:4). Teamwork requires that they learn how to "be subordinate to one another out of reverence for Christ" (Eph 5:21). Mutual submission is the only sure way to build lasting unity in marriage and to foster the kind of communion that permeates the entire family and creates a secure environment for everyone.

When these four areas of communion and healthy communication are present in marriage, trust and fidelity replace fear and unfaithfulness. From this base of unity, couples naturally desire to express their love for one another totally—body, soul, and spirit—in sexual intimacy. I have noticed through my years of counseling married couples and conducting marriage conferences, as well as in my own marriage, that sexual intimacy thrives in an environment of trust, where couples are faithful and secure, spiritually united, emotionally intimate, enjoying time with each other outside the bedroom, and willing to work together as a team in solving problems and making decisions. When these conditions are present, lovemaking becomes a beautiful and deeply satisfying expression of their communion in the Holy Spirit with one another.

The converse is also true. Married couples who have not established trust and unity in the first four areas of intimacy often lose interest in sexual intimacy or find it to be a source of great conflict or disappointment in their relationship. As a response, they may give themselves only partially to one another, offering their body but withholding their heart and soul. They need to first heal the other areas of communion before being able to offer themselves freely and fully.

Couples who cultivate all five of these areas of communion are blessedly happy because they remain in communion with God, who is eternal blessedness. God's intimate and faithful love heals the wounds of fear that may have accumulated over years of hurt in the family of origin or in dating relationships prior to marriage. Even when trust has been damaged in the earlier years of marriage, fear bonds can be transformed into love bonds by inviting Jesus into the marriage and into those areas where we have been wounded in the past.

Holy marriages like this become a light to the world. When husbands and wives humbly and selflessly serve one another and seek the will of God in their lives, they become a compelling witness to other married couples. This witness overflows to those who are not yet married, including their children, friends, relatives, and the world. The world is starving for this kind of perfect love, which "drives out fear" (1 Jn 4:18). Of course only God's love is perfect, but marriage is supposed to be the living witness to his love for all to see. For this we all need to be continually transformed so that our love becomes a true reflection of the love of Christ. This is the true meaning of marriage as a sacrament. Grounded in Christ, and filled with his faithful and intimate love, it creates a loving family atmosphere in the home where all the members can grow in their true identity and participate in his mission of bringing all people back into his loving embrace.

—∽—

Over the years, I have been privileged to observe many couples undergo transformation in their marital relationships as they learn the true meaning of the sacrament and do the sometimes hard work of putting this into practice through the five areas of communion. One of the most remarkable ongoing transformations is from a couple on our ministry team, John and Krista. A few years ago, they courageously shared their story at one of our *Unveiled* marriage conferences. Many of the couples attending were touched by their honesty and vulnerability. Recently they gave me permission to share their story with you. Their witness is an inspiring illustration of how communion can grow over time when we turn our hearts toward God in trust.

When I first met John and Krista they were both suffering tremendously. As a result of their own individual wounds and self-protections, their marriage was lacking in all five areas of communion. None of the five were present to any significant degree as they had tremendous amounts of mistrust after struggling with many forms of unfaithfulness early in their marriage. For differing reasons, their childhood homes lacked secure love, so neither of them brought a capacity for genuine love into the marriage. They both entered their relationship with layers of hidden fear and mistrust. Though they both grew up in culturally "Christian" homes, neither of them knew Jesus in a way that made a difference in how they interacted on a daily basis. Nor did they have any good examples of what a good marriage, rooted and grounded in Christ's love, could look like. Both of their parents' marriages had been continually conflicted, with Krista's parents eventually divorcing. Needless to say, their childhood experiences and early marriage did not afford a good foundation of trust for a blessed marriage.

After a tumultuous dating relationship, John and Krista decided to marry after getting pregnant with their daughter. Though they were married in a church, they had no concept for marriage as a sacrament except for the desires written in each of their hearts to be loved and cherished for a lifetime. Infidelity and mistrust became constant impediments to these desires, until they both finally gave up and divorced after a few years of tearing each other to pieces by their endless conflicts, accusations, and emotional withdrawals.

As much as they regretted the pain they caused their daughter and each other, God worked through this difficult time of separation. Three months after divorcing, they remarried at the courthouse. But in less than a year, things started falling apart again because neither of them had faced their underlying wounds and identity lies or the reasons for earlier failures. They each lacked a solid foundation of trust and a genuine capacity to love one another faithfully and fully.

But this time, instead of giving up again, they each began searching for genuine love and found what they had been searching for their entire life in the person of Jesus. Once they truly encountered him and surrendered their lives to him, they each discovered a renewed sense of hope. Unfortunately the honeymoon only lasted a short time. Fear bonds continued to prevent them from making much progress in building communion in their marriage. Though their faith kept them from divorcing again, they were both still very deeply wounded and responded to each other out of self-protection and mutual mistrust.

Things finally began to change in their marital dynamics when both of them seriously invested themselves in seeking healing for their many wounds that had accumulated over years of childhood, dating, and marriage. This challenging but rewarding process prepared their hearts for a few major transformations. First, Jesus met each of them in very tender ways in the areas of their childhood hurt. Then, during a class on Christian marriage they volunteered to say their vows as a part of a demonstration in front of the rest of the class. At the beginning of the demonstration they were both joking around, not taking it seriously, but as soon as they began to enact the wedding ceremony the Holy Spirit quickly turned the occasion into a powerful time of vulnerability and relational healing.

Gazing intently into each other's eyes, first John and then Krista slowly and intentionally spoke their vows to one another. As they did, tears welled up in each of their eyes and they could see and feel that Jesus was the bond of love holding their marriage together. They understood deeply for the first time that they had entered into a sacred covenant and not a contract. At that moment, Jesus truly became the center of their marriage. The awareness of his presence in their marriage changed everything. They began trusting God and each other with a new confidence, finally believing that they would be devoted to faithfully loving each other for the rest of their lives. Two weeks after renewing their vows, God gave them another incredible gift. Following eleven years of struggling with secondary infertility, they became pregnant with their second child, this time a little boy.

As their love has matured over the subsequent years, their fears and fighting have lessened significantly. They are growing in all five areas of marital communion, and their marriage has become fruitful in ways they could not have imagined. Soon after the birth of their son, they became foster parents. To date, they have invited more than fifty children into their family and shared the healing love of Jesus with them as well as the children's wounded parents whenever possible. Recently, John and Krista adopted five of these foster children and now have a beautiful family of seven children ranging in age from one year old to twenty-two years old. Today, Jesus shines through their sacrament. Many are blessed by their love, not the least of which are these precious children who have found a secure home where they can come to know God's faithful love. Things are not perfect. But with his faithful and secure love as the bedrock of their marriage, they are now able to negotiate even the bumpy times with considerably more grace.

Isn't this what we all desire—to love and be loved faithfully and securely, grounded in a heartfelt communion with God and one another? Only love like this can heal our wounds of fear and mistrust that plague all of us (on this side of Eden) in one way or another. Let's stop here and reflect on all we have discussed, and then enter in more personally through prayer and scripture to follow.

Take a Moment

1. If you are married, assess the five areas of communion in your relationship. If you are not married, assess these five areas in your parents' marriage and home life growing up.

2. How does the sacrament of Matrimony build bonds of trust and unity? How does this heal wounds of fear and mistrust? How was this illustrated in John and Krista's story? Be specific.

Scripture Meditation

The following passage from 1 Corinthians 13 is one that many couples choose for their wedding to express the love they desire to embody in their marriage. It applies to all good relationships. I encourage you to reflect on this passage, asking the Holy Spirit for revelation.

1. As you read it the first time, I encourage you to put "I" in every time the word "love" or "it" appears in the text. So, for example, rather than "Love is patient, love is kind, it is not jealous," say, "I am patient, I am kind, I am not jealous." Say it out loud. Make note of where the words ring true and where they seem empty or less true.

2. The second time through, instead of your name, place Jesus' name in the place of "love" or "it." "Jesus is patient, Jesus is kind. . . . Jesus is not quick-tempered . . . Jesus does not brood over injury." See if that rings true to you. Then examine the gap between you and Jesus. Don't allow yourself to become discouraged where you fall short or become proud where you love well.

3. With the third time reading it, place both you and Jesus in the passage as one: "Jesus in me is patient, Jesus in me is kind" and so on. This third time will help you see the reality of living in your true identity in Christ as his sacrament of love. This kind of love is

faithful and helps us to build deep and lasting communion, which in turn allows us to feel deeply secure.

Faithful Love

"Love is patient, love is kind. It is not jealous, [love] is not pompous, it is not inflated, it is not rude, it does not seek its own interests, it is not quick-tempered, it does not brood over injury, it does not rejoice over wrongdoing but rejoices with the truth. It bears all things, believes all things, hopes all things, endures all things. Love never fails" (1 Cor 13:4–8).

Let Us Pray

As we have discussed, fear and mistrust are obstacles to communion and faithfulness in marriage. In this prayer experience, I invite you to explore this in your own life, with the help of the Holy Spirit, so you can grow in your capacity to love.

1. Ask the Holy Spirit to show you your weaknesses in living out 1 Corinthians 13. Write down the areas where you are weakest or struggle the most (impatience, jealousy, meanness, selfishness, quick temper, hopelessness, and so forth).

2. Then ask the Holy Spirit to show you where wounds of *fear and mistrust* are underneath these areas of unfaithfulness.

3. Next, invite the Holy Spirit to show you where these wounds originate in your life, through lack of security in your relationships.

4. Finally, ask Jesus to reveal his love to you in those specific areas where there is lack and to give his grace in those places of need. Record in a journal what you receive in prayer.

8

PURE AND UNDEFILED

How Reconciliation Heals Wounds of Shame

*Neither do I condemn you. Go, and from now
on do not sin any more.*

John 8:11

As a young girl, Serena sat in the darkened church while her uncle went to confession. She had no way of knowing whether her uncle confessed "that secret sin" to the priest and, if he did, why the priest never did anything to stop it and get him thrown into jail. Time after time, she sat there as he went to confession and then waited for the next time he would sexually molest her. Since nothing changed after his confessions, Serena concluded the priest's "forgiveness" was just an excuse for her uncle to do it again without guilt.

By the time I met Serena, she was married and had her own children. The nightmare of her molestation was long over, but the debilitating shadows were still very much present. She continued carrying the toxic shame of her sexual abuse around with her and constantly battled the sins that sprang from it. Her critical comments about confession indicated that she saw the sacrament as a cover-up for sin. Once I heard the details of her story, I could appreciate the reasons for her contempt for the sacrament and the depths of pain buried beneath her misconceptions.

At one point she asked me if I thought it was okay that the priest forgave her uncle's sexual abuse while he kept doing it. (I later found out her mother had justified and denied her uncle's abusive behavior.) I told her that forgiveness does not justify any sin and especially one as damaging as sexual abuse. I added that I had no way of knowing whether her uncle confessed this particular sin, or did so with a contrite heart, but if he confessed in humility, the priest was there as a representative of Jesus to reveal God's mercy (see *CCC*, 1442 and 1461).

I added that the priest was bound by confidentiality under the "sacramental seal," so he could not report the abuse even if it was confessed (see *CCC*, 1467). That certainly did not mean God or the priest *excused* her uncle's sin or didn't care about what happened to her. Jesus' death on the cross shows how much God hates sin and yet loves all of us sinners. To emphasize this point, I shared with her Jesus' warning regarding those who harm little ones: "Whoever causes one of these little ones who believe in me to sin, it would be better for him to have a great millstone hung around his neck and to be drowned in the depths of the sea. Woe to the world because of things that cause sin! Such things must come, but woe to the one through whom they come" (Mt 18:6–7).

Serena received several things in this passage that both comforted and challenged her. She seemed consoled to find out that God hated every evil thing that happened to her and did not take it lightly. She also realized that many of her sins had been precipitated by the abuse. Though she was still responsible for her sins, she was comforted to know that God understood where many of those thoughts and behaviors in her life originated. In facing all this, she also acknowledged that maybe her uncle's sin had been partly brought on by abuse he suffered also. She realized she needed to forgive her uncle if she expected to be forgiven (see Mt 6:14–15). But, it would take her many years of therapy and healing before she was able to do this from the depths of her heart. Layers of hurt and degradation kept her heart bound in shame.

For a long time, Serena could not meet my eyes. Her shame, from the sexual abuse and her own sins, kept her believing the lie that she was bad and dirty. It crippled nearly every aspect of her life, including her intimacy with her husband, her relationship with her children, and most importantly, her relationship with God.

—ᜰᜰ—

Whether or not we can relate to Serena's experience, all of us struggle with shame in our lives to one degree or another. Though our circumstances and awareness may vary dramatically, we all know the experience of feeling unworthy and wanting to hide what we fear might be met by others' judgment and condemnation. Whether we realize it or not, shame interferes with our relationships with God, ourselves, and others.

Shame is generally understood as a consciousness of sin or shortcoming resulting in a condition of dishonor or disgrace.[1] To understand its origins, we need to go back to the beginning of human history where this deadly wound first took hold in the hearts of Adam and Eve when they covered themselves and hid from God after violating his commandments.

As we know, Adam and Eve began their life in a state of perpetual grace, fully participating in the inner life of God. All of their actions were done according to justice because they trusted God and submitted to his will in every aspect of their daily life. As long as they continued in communion with God, they remained pure and undefiled, in a state that St. John Paul II refers to as "original innocence."[2]

The instant Adam and Eve succumbed to the father of lies they lost their innocence. At that moment, shame arose in their consciousness as they moved out of a state of grace and into *dis-grace*. Immediately, they became self-conscious and began to cover themselves, recognizing they no longer felt safe to be seen as they were in their deficiency: "Then the eyes of both of them were opened, and they knew that they were naked; so they sewed fig leaves together and made loincloths for themselves." After covering themselves, they hid again—this time from God (Gn 3:7–8).

In his commentary on this passage, St. John Paul II draws our attention to the freedom and intimacy Adam and Eve experienced before shame entered the picture: "They see and know each other, in fact, with all the peace of the interior gaze, which creates precisely the fullness of intimacy of persons."[3] This is what we all long for, isn't it? To be seen and known and loved, without pretensions and without the fear of condemnation. Sadly, shame interferes with this deepest need and desire.

—⁂—

Do you recognize what is at stake here with the onset of sin and shame? Our core identity is threatened. God created each one of us to be *pure and undefiled* in a state of original innocence to participate in his inner life of holiness and to enjoy continuing intimacy with him and with one another. However, sin and shame cuts us off from communion; we end up covering ourselves so that others won't see and know our dis-grace. We lose a measure of our capacity to participate in God's inner life (his grace) in every area of our being where shame has a hold on us.

As we saw in Serena's situation, shame has many faces. There is a healthy side to shame, which is a consciousness of our sin as deficiency, or loss of grace. The antithesis would be "shamelessness." Throughout the scriptures that word is used to describe people who have completely disregarded God's justice and are setting themselves up for destruction (see Zep 2, Jude 1:13). Serena's uncle's apparent lack of repentance reveals his shamelessness, but perhaps his going to confession showed there was some inkling of "healthy" shame in his life. We may never know on this side of heaven.

Shame, in this positive sense, is awareness that we have moved out of purity and communion and that there is some part of our lives that is defiled and in a state of dis-grace. When responded to in humility, this kind of shame leads us to repentance and confession, as the Holy Spirit convicts us of sin and God's righteousness (see Jn 16:8). Serena felt shame over her own sin and knew she needed God's mercy, forgiveness, and restoration. But this healthy sense of her shame was clouded by a "toxic shame" resulting from her abuse and other wounds in her life.

Toxic shame is debilitating in many ways. Serena's abuse left her feeling "dirty and unlovable." She felt disgraced and dishonored by what her uncle did to her and then subsequently by her own thoughts and behaviors. When these areas of shame were not addressed in her life, she saw herself as an inferior human being, believing she was tarnished and defective and condemning herself for her existence.

As a young girl, Serena didn't have the words to describe what happened to her. But we can imagine her experience as we listen to King David's daughter Tamar express how she felt to be violated by her half-brother Amnon: "'No, my brother! Do not force me! This is not done in Israel. Do not commit this terrible crime. Where would I take my shame? And you would be labeled a fool in Israel.' . . . But he would not listen to her; he was too strong for her: he forced her down and raped her. . . . Tamar put ashes on her head and tore the long tunic in which she was clothed. Then, putting her hands to her head, she went away crying loudly" (2 Sm 13:12–14, 19).

I appreciate the rawness of the scriptures. We are invited right into Tamar's anguish while she describes the heartbreaking shame both she and Amnon would experience. Tamar's words and subsequent actions highlight Serena's and her uncle's shame as well. Both victim and victimizer were horribly scarred by this violation of their human dignity. Only one of them sinned and needed to repent, but both of them experienced disgrace and each of them needed God's merciful love and healing to restore them to wholeness.

God's mercy is the only known remedy for our shame. And the sacrament of Reconciliation is one of the Church's primary means of communicating this incredible and completely underserved gift of God's compassion and forgiveness. Through the sacrament, the Holy Spirit is capable of reaching the deepest areas of our heart that keep us in degradation and separation. "The whole power of the sacrament of Penance [Reconciliation] consists in restoring us to God's grace and joining us with him in an intimate friendship" (*CCC*, 1468). As such it heals the wounds of shame (dis-grace) and restores us to our true identity in Christ, as pure and undefiled children of the Father (see 1 Jn 3:1–3).

The full restoration of our identity is a lifelong process where God's light penetrates and dispels the darkness of our sin and shame. John in his letter to the churches explains:

> God is light, and in him there is no darkness at all. If we say, "We have fellowship with him," while we continue to walk in darkness, we lie and do not act in truth. But if we walk in the light as he is in the light, then we have fellowship with one another, and the blood of his son Jesus cleanses us from all sin. If we say, "We are without sin," we deceive ourselves, and the truth is not in us. If we acknowledge our sins, he is faithful and just and will forgive our sins and cleanse us from every wrongdoing. If we say, "We have not sinned," we make him a liar and his word is not in us. (1 Jn 1:5–10)

Notice these four primary activities involved in being restored to purity, which St. John mentions, and how they describe the process involved in the sacrament of Reconciliation:

1. We acknowledge our sins (confession).
2. We are forgiven (absolution).
3. We are cleansed (deliverance).
4. We are restored to fellowship to walk in the light (penance/ reparation for our sins/healing).

Commenting on this process, Fr. Raniero Cantalamessa observes, "The Holy Spirit is the remission of all sins." He convicts us of our sins, and then "carries out the work of purification in us from deep within our inmost being . . . melts our stony-hard heart . . . and remolds us in the image of God."[4] Fr. Cantalamessa adds that this process is articulated beautifully in the Syriac Church when the priest speaks words of absolution: "May the Lord, by the inrushing of the Holy Spirit, destroy and utterly wipe out of your soul every fault, every blasphemy, and every kind of injustice by which your soul has been made unclean."[5]

What powerful imagery: the "inrushing of the Holy Spirit" gives a visual image of God's love and light rushing in through a recently opened portal to the heart. Words like "destroy" and "wipe out" speak of total destruction of sin that happens with the sacrament. Can you hear in this description how the sacrament of Reconciliation is intended not only for our forgiveness but also for our purification and healing? "Every injustice by which your soul has been made unclean" speaks to the impurity and injustice that result from sin and the process of purification that is necessary.

Contrary to Serena's experience and misperception, God's mercy does not disregard justice and holiness but becomes the only truly effective means for restoring these virtues. God forgives us not to excuse our sin but to restore us to wholeness. His goal is our full restoration in justice and innocence so that we can become "pure and undefiled" in communion with Jesus. This is God's work in us, through the cleansing blood of Jesus and the Holy Spirit "rushing in" through the sacrament.

Let's pause here to reflect on this amazing gift of God's merciful love flowing through the sacrament of Reconciliation, meeting us in the places of our deepest misery and disgrace.

Take a Moment

1. When are you most aware of shame in your life? How does it break your intimacy with God and others? How is your own integrity affected?

2. How have you encountered the Father's mercy in Confession/Reconciliation?

3. Describe the four-part process of healing through the sacrament of Reconciliation. How have you experienced each step in the process?

4. Do you believe there is sin so hideous that it is beyond God's
    mercy? Explain.

—∞—

Question number four is one we all have to ask ourselves personally
because our answer reveals the areas we will refuse to forgive and
receive forgiveness in our lives and thus hold on to our shame and
condemnation. Have you done anything that you believe God can't
forgive? What have others done to you that you believe is unforgivable? What Serena's uncle did was atrocious. Do you believe it was
an "unforgivable sin" and beyond God's mercy?

Jesus answered these questions for us when he died on the cross
and gave us the sacraments so that God's mercy could be received
by every person who seeks it with true contrition. Speaking words of
forgiveness from the cross, in the face of the worst injustice in all of
history, he showed that nothing was outside of God's mercy—with
only one exception. Do you know what that exception is?

Jesus tells us plainly: we cannot be forgiven if we eternally refuse
to acknowledge our sin and if we show contempt for God's mercy.
This is what Jesus meant when he spoke about "blasphemy of the
Holy Spirit" (see Mk 3:29). Though often misunderstood, blasphemy
of the Holy Spirit is an extreme hardness of heart, where a person is
so entrenched and self-justified in his sin that he permanently and
eternally refuses to recognize God's justice or his own need for God's
mercy. This was the sin of many of the Pharisees who killed Jesus.
Jesus forgave them, but they may or may not have received his mercy,
depending on their willingness to repent.

Was Serena's uncle guilty of this kind of unrepentant hardness? I
don't know, but I hope not. I pray for him. I do believe that if he had
any inkling of his sin and shame, the Church would offer Christ's
forgiveness to him through the sacrament of Reconciliation. Would
that be fair to Serena? Does the Church even care about her healing?

—∞—

According to the *Catechism*, the sacrament of Reconciliation is not only intended for the healing of the penitent but also for the benefit of all those harmed by his sin. Full reconciliation requires that we do all we can for our own restoration as well as the restoration of those harmed.

Here is a synopsis of what the Church teaches in this regard: "Many sins wrong our neighbor. One must do what is possible to repair the harm (e.g., return stolen goods, restore the reputation of someone slandered, pay compensation for injuries). Simple justice requires as much. But sin also injures and weakens the sinner himself, as well as his relationships with God and neighbor. Absolution takes away sin, but it does not remedy all the disorders sin has caused. Raised up from sin, the sinner must still recover his spiritual health by doing something more to make amends for his sin . . . this satisfaction is also called penance" (*CCC*, 1459).

In *Reconciliation and Penance*, St. John Paul II adds, "This reconciliation with God leads, as it were, to other reconciliations, which repair the other breaches caused by sin. The forgiven penitent is reconciled with himself in his inmost being, where he regains his innermost truth. He is reconciled with his brethren whom he has in some way offended and wounded. He is reconciled with the Church. He is reconciled with all creation."[6]

Can you see how the sacrament of Reconciliation is intended to bring healing, first to the repentant sinner, and then through him to all those affected by his sin? The Church is wise, because it is directed by the Holy Spirit and keeps its eyes always focused on our full restoration and fulfillment.

Can you imagine how different things would be for Serena and her uncle if he would have pursued Serena's restoration as well as his own? Sound far-fetched? It's not. I have witnessed this kind of reconciliation many times in many different circumstances. The following amazing reconciliation, in a somewhat similar situation, left a lasting impression upon me, showing that God can do unimaginable things when we turn to him. The family you are about to meet truly entered into reconciliation and with it experienced deep and lasting healing for everyone involved.

The mother of the family, Danielle, was overwhelmed with grief and rage as she struggled to share why she came for help. She had recently separated from Hank, her husband of thirty-eight years, after finding out that he had been sexually abusing their four daughters throughout their childhood. Danielle was horrified as she struggled to face the torment and disgrace that had ravaged their family. She had loved Hank since they were both young; now all she wanted to do was kill him. Her murderous rage is what led her to separate and move to another state, so that she did not end up doing something she would later regret.

Danielle's healing process began slowly at first but accelerated rapidly as she frequented the sacrament of Reconciliation. There she would regularly confess her rage as well as her own shame and guilt over not seeing the clues of the abuse over the years so she could protect her daughters. She felt personally humiliated and felt even more troubled for her daughters' humiliation and anguish. When it was happening, she buried her head in the sand, but now everything finally made sense of her daughters' problems: drug abuse, ill-advised relationships, estrangement, self-harming, perfectionism, unmanageable anxiety, and suicidal depression.

But now it was time for Danielle to heal so that she eventually could bring healing to her broken family. As she cried out to God in her distress, an amazing thing happened over a sixth-month period. Partly as a fruit of her regularly participating in the sacraments of Reconciliation and daily Eucharist and partly due to her healing process in therapy, Danielle slowly moved from rage to compassion for Hank. Having received God's mercy herself, she desired for Hank to receive forgiveness before he died. She did not want him to go to hell. She began to pray earnestly. Within a few months she felt led to encourage Hank to take a leave of absence from work, so that he could engage in his own healing process.

Hank was convinced that he was beyond God's mercy. And his children readily agreed. At first they were furious with their mother for extending compassion because they thought she was continuing to enable him. But eventually they had a change of heart, as they heard reports of their father's willingness to repent and face what he had done to them. Like Danielle, Hank took a big step forward when he went to the sacrament of Reconciliation and confessed his sins. After the confession, a sliver of light broke through into the darkness that had permeated his soul. It was an important step in his moving from disgrace to grace, but he was still far from releasing the majority of his toxic shame and entering into communion with God or anyone else.

Hank struggled intensely as he tried to face and come to terms with all the ways he had betrayed his wife and done untold damage to his children. He saw himself as a monster. His favorite verse from scripture at the time was the one I had shown Serena about the millstone: "Whoever causes one of these little ones who believe in me to sin, it would be better for him to have a great millstone hung around his neck and to be drowned in the depths of the sea" (Mt 18:6). His shame and self-hatred reached such intensity that he longed to have a millstone put around his neck so that he could be drowned in the sea. That, he believed, is what he deserved and the only way he would find any relief.

Even after his confession, Hank did not believe he was worthy of God's mercy. When I spoke to him about accepting Jesus' forgiveness and compassion, he would retort, "I cannot do that until my children and wife are healed and they can forgive me." I admired his desire to sacrifice his good for their sake, but I tried to explain to him that we needed to start with him and his relationship with God. Only then could he help bring healing to the rest of the family. Otherwise he would still be using them to get something (approval) he needed from them.

One saving grace is that Hank was willing to look at himself in the mirror through the scriptures. One particular day, we were led to the story of the woman caught in adultery in the Gospel of John. The entire story is about Jesus meeting the woman in the place of her humiliation and disgrace. When everyone else condemned her, Jesus showed the Father's heart of love and mercy. I asked Hank if I could read this to him and place his name everywhere it spoke about the woman interacting with Jesus. I encouraged him to invite the Holy Spirit to speak to his heart through it all. After some initial resistance, he consented.

Having received the sacrament of Reconciliation earlier that week, these four statements from Jesus, through the scriptures, pierced Hank's heart:

"Let the one among you who is without sin be the first to throw a stone at [Hank]" (Jn 8:7).

"[Hank], . . . has no one condemned you? . . . Neither do I condemn you" (Jn 8:10–11).

"[Hank,] go, and from now on do not sin any more" (Jn 8:11).

"I am the light of the world. [Hank, if you] follow me, [you] will not walk in darkness, but will have the light of life" (Jn 8:12).

In hearing Jesus speak directly to him through the scripture, Hank finally *received* the grace of the sacrament that had been offered to him a few days earlier. He realized that all the accusations inside his mind were stones that he was constantly throwing at himself and imagining that his daughters and wife were also throwing at him. He finally believed that Jesus was not condemning him. He had been condemning himself all along, while Jesus was reaching out to him, first through his wife and then through the priest, to restore him to grace and wholeness. With a new awareness of God's mercy, he finally understood the call to repentance and received it for the first time with hope: he would take up Jesus' admonition to sin no more and to follow him as a disciple so he could walk in the light and not in the darkness.

Up until this moment, my words could not convince Hank that the Father had extended his hands of mercy and forgiveness. Jesus' words through the sacrament and then later through the scriptures became the living and effective word that prompted his conversion. God's Word and sacrament are able to penetrate our hearts through the Holy Spirit like nothing else, especially when we approach him in prayer (see Heb 4:12, Jas 5:16–18).

With this breakthrough in his ability to receive the Father's mercy, Hank began to heal rapidly. His wife, Danielle, could see the changes and eventually trusted the genuineness of his conversion. They began to meet, in and out of therapy, to work through their many issues, and then, one at a time, Hank invited each of his daughters to come to therapy with him, so that he could apologize and reconcile with each of them.[7] He invited each of them to share anything they wanted and gave them freedom to relive the events in their memory, and in doing so to express their anger, hurt, shame, outrage, and so forth.

Because Hank had his identity more firmly rooted in the Father, he could withstand all the accusations, most of which he knew were true. He simply agreed and with deep anguish felt compassion for all the pain he had caused his daughters. Their sharing helped him have genuine contrition for his sin (see 2 Cor 7:9–11). When his daughters were ready, he and Danielle helped them each work through their pain and shame. Hank found great fulfillment in finally being able to love his daughters in a way that was for their good, rather than using them for his own selfish purposes as he had done for years. In the end, the daughters could each forgive their dad and mom from their hearts.

About ten years after these events, Danielle came back to town for a visit and requested to meet with me. She was glowing. She couldn't wait to tell me about the amazing healing and reconciliation that had taken place in their family. After moving back to their city, she and Hank moved into their home together and each of the children began to come for longer visits. Some lived with them for a time, and others brought their children around. The trust had been restored to such an extent that the daughters were freely affectionate with both their dad and mom and allowed their children to interact with each of them freely. Shame no longer had a stranglehold on Hank or their family.

During our meeting, Danielle told me that Hank had died two years earlier and that she felt confident she would meet him in heaven one day. She marveled that the years before he died had been the happiest time they had ever experienced together as a family. Shame and humiliation gave way to a beautiful intimacy and communion. She never believed this could be possible after all the devastation they had experienced as a family. Deeply grateful to God for restoring them, she wept as she told me all the beautiful things that happened in their family. She knew only Jesus could do something like this: "And all this is from God, who has reconciled us to himself through Christ and given us the ministry of reconciliation" (2 Cor 5:18).

The changes in Danielle and Hank began and deepened with the sacrament of Reconciliation. Through their individual reconciliations with God and the Church, Danielle and then Hank became ministers of reconciliation first to each other and then with their daughters. They also had to reconcile with their extended family members who were deeply hurt by the knowledge of the abuse. They each took responsibility for their part, asked for forgiveness, and did everything they possibly could to restore their daughters, their families, and each other.

Experiences like these help to remind all of us that "the gospel is the revelation in Jesus Christ of God's mercy to sinners" (*CCC*, 1846). The priesthood is the face of Christ, serving as the frontline ministers of reconciliation in the Church. The ordained priesthood reveals God's mercy in a very direct way through the sacrament (see Jas 5:14–16).[8] The rest of us are also priests (mediators) in Christ, called to first receive his mercy and then to reveal his forgiveness to the world around us. In this sense, we are all ministers of reconciliation, healing the wounds of shame caused by sin (see 2 Cor 5:18–19). Everything starts with Christ's death and resurrection. The graces flow from there through the sacrament of Reconciliation, and then these graces must be lived in every aspect of our lives.

The following reflection questions, scripture meditation, and prayer experience are intended to help you receive these graces more fully in your life.

Take a Moment

1. Have you ever been in Danielle's shoes and been able to extend mercy to someone who hurt you deeply? Did the sacrament of Reconciliation play a role in that? How?

2. How did Hank's repentance differ from that of Serena's uncle? How did he become a minister of reconciliation for all those whom he had hurt?

3. When did Hank receive God's mercy? When was it granted?

4. In what area of your life do you need to hear that Jesus does not condemn you? Are you willing to let go of your shame and receive his mercy?

5. Where is God calling you to be his minister of reconciliation?

Scripture Meditation

The following passage is the one that I read to Hank from John 8 regarding Jesus and the woman caught in adultery. I encourage you to enter your name in the place of the woman, as we did with Hank.

1. Ask the Holy Spirit to guide you as you reflect on the scripture passage.

2. Read the passage slowly the first time through for overall understanding.

3. Read a second time slowly, placing your name in the place of the woman; allow yourself to feel the shame and then experience Jesus' response.

4. Read a third time, very slowly, allowing the Holy Spirit to speak to you through the passage. Write down what you receive.

Jesus and the Woman Caught in Adultery

"Then the scribes and the Pharisees brought a woman who had been caught in adultery and made her stand in the middle. They said to him, 'Teacher, this woman was caught in the very act of committing adultery. Now in the law, Moses commanded us to stone such women. So what do you say?' They said this to test him, so that they could have some charge to bring against him. Jesus bent down and began to write on the ground with his finger. But when they continued asking him, he straightened up and said to them, 'Let the one among you who is without sin be the first to throw a stone at her.' Again he bent down and wrote on the ground. And in response, they went away one by one, beginning with the elders. So he was left alone with the woman before him. Then Jesus straightened up and said to her, 'Woman, where are they? Has no one condemned you?' She replied, 'No one, sir.' Then Jesus said, 'Neither do I condemn you. Go, [and] from now on do not sin anymore.' Jesus spoke to them again, saying, 'I am the light of the world. Whoever follows me will not walk in darkness, but will have the light of life'" (Jn 8:3–12).

Let Us Pray

The following is King David's prayer of repentance after the prophet Nathan confronted him regarding his adultery with Bathsheba and the murder of her husband, Uriah. Jesus taught that we commit adultery anytime we lust in our hearts or are unfaithful to God in some way and we murder whenever we hold resentment or slander someone (see Mt 5:21–30, Jas 4:4). Think of a time when you were unfaithful in some way or hurt someone through your anger or vengeance. Then pray this prayer from your heart to the Father imploring his mercy. Following this prayer, if you have access to the sacrament of Reconciliation, I encourage you to confess these sins to a priest and to hear Jesus speak to you (through his representative) that your sins are forgiven. If you do not have the opportunity to receive the sacrament, I encourage you to practice the four steps of reconciliation (from page 124), confessing to someone you trust. (These four steps of reconciliation represent the core teaching and practice of the twelve-step recovery process that began with Alcoholics Anonymous.)

Prayer of Repentance

"Have mercy on me, God, in accord with your merciful love; in your abundant compassion blot out my transgressions.

"Thoroughly wash away my guilt; and from my sin cleanse me.

"For I know my transgressions; my sin is always before me.

"Against you, you alone have I sinned; I have done what is evil in your eyes. So that you are just in your word, and without reproach in your judgment. Behold, I was born in guilt, in sin my mother conceived me. Behold, you desire true sincerity; and secretly you teach me wisdom.

"Cleanse me with hyssop that I may be pure; wash me, and I will be whiter than snow. You will let me hear gladness and joy; the bones you have crushed will rejoice.

"Turn away your face from my sins; blot out all my iniquities.

"A clean heart create for me, God; renew within me a steadfast spirit.

"Do not drive me from before your face, nor take from me your holy spirit.

"Restore to me the gladness of your salvation; uphold me with a willing spirit. I will teach the wicked your ways, that sinners may return to you . . .

"My sacrifice, O God, is a contrite spirit; a contrite, humbled heart, O God, you will not scorn" (Ps 51:3–15, 19).

9

RAISED TO LIFE

How the Anointing of the Sick Heals
Wounds of Hopelessness

The kingdom of heaven is at hand.
Cure the sick, raise the dead.

Matthew 10:7–8

On every Easter Sunday, Christian churches throughout the world joyfully proclaim with one voice this central tenet of our faith: *Christ is risen from the dead! Alleluia!* Jesus' resurrection is the cause of our joy and the basis for our enduring hope in the promise of eternal life (see 1 Cor 15:1, 1 Thes 4:13, Tt 1:2, 1 Pt 1:3). Without it, St. Paul tells us, our faith is in vain (see 1 Cor 15:17). That is why the resurrection from the dead holds central place in all our creeds. By professing a belief in Jesus' resurrection, we affirm that Jesus is alive and in our midst and that each of us will experience our own personal resurrection from the dead. This is an anchor of hope for every one of us.

All the sacraments derive their limitless power from Jesus' resurrection, each in its own unique way (see *CCC*, 1091). The sacrament of the Anointing of the Sick specifically confronts sickness, hopelessness, and death. In turn, Jesus' resurrection power is actualized in three distinct ways: (1) by providing strength and hope in the midst of illness; (2) through restoring our health; and (3) by preparing us for our final glorification, where we will be made completely whole (see *CCC*, 1532). "By the sacred anointing of the sick and the prayer of the priests, the whole Church commends those who are ill to the suffering and glorified Lord, that he may *raise them up* and save them" (*CCC*, 1499, emphasis added).

Sickness brings us face to face with death and hopelessness: "Every illness can make us glimpse death" (*CCC*, 1500). "Illness can lead to anguish, self-absorption, sometimes even despair [i.e., hopelessness]" (*CCC*, 1501). Conversely, every healing encounter with the risen Lord reveals a glimpse of the glory of his resurrection life. The Roman Rite for the Anointing of the Sick speaks of this reality: "Through this holy anointing may the Lord in his love and mercy help you with the grace of the Holy Spirit. May the Lord, who frees you from sin, save you and *raise you up*."[1]

Notice the words "raise you up" in the descriptions and prayers for this sacrament. They are an allusion to the resurrection and are reminiscent of similar references by the authors of the New Testament when speaking of Jesus' healing ministry. First, Matthew observes, "Jesus entered the house of Peter, and saw his mother-in-law lying in bed with a fever. He touched her hand, the fever left her, and *she rose* and waited on him" (Mt 8:14–15, emphasis added).

Similarly, St. James adds, "Is anyone among you sick? He should summon the presbyters of the church, and they should pray over him and anoint him with oil in the name of the Lord, and the prayer of faith will save the sick person, and the Lord will *raise him up*. If he has committed any sins, he will be forgiven" (Jas 5:14–15, emphasis added). This passage from James reveals the rudimentary form of the sacrament of the Anointing of the Sick in the earliest days of the Church. This sacrament is a sign of Christ's resurrection life healing us now and a prefiguring of the final resurrection where we will be made completely whole. On that final day, we will be "raised to life" and our identity completely restored and made new, in him.

—⚬〰⚬—

Jesus' resurrection is the promise and fulfillment of all God purposed for us when he created us: a life full of hope and health, free from sickness, death, and despair. Before sin entered the world, sickness and death did not exist. Neither did hopelessness, which is the wound most closely associated with sickness and death. Like each of the other wounds that we have been exploring throughout this book, hopelessness took hold in the human heart with Adam and Eve's disobedience and separation from God.

God instructed them, "You are free to eat from any of the trees of the garden except the tree of knowledge of good and evil. From that tree you shall not eat; when you eat from it you shall die" (Gn 2:16–17). Challenging the Father's integrity, the father of lies countered, "You certainly will not die!" (Gn 3:4). The serpent then proceeded to accuse God of withholding something good from our first parents.[2] We all know the rest of the story. Cutting themselves off from the source of all genuine and lasting hope, Adam and Eve doomed themselves and the rest of the human race to the curses of death and hopelessness.

For a brief time it may have seemed to Adam and Eve that they escaped the curse of death because they didn't immediately drop dead, at least physically. But as they would soon discover, the seeds of death and hopelessness entered their lives precisely at the very moment they separated themselves from the Father.[3] Their spiritual death eventually manifested in physical death. In between their spiritual and physical deaths, they subjected themselves and the entire human race to diseases and distresses of every form and fashion, all evidences of death's stranglehold over creation.

From the instant sin entered the world, all of creation was doomed to a hopeless death. In our own lives, sin mysteriously ushers doom, disease, and despair into our bodies and souls (all symptoms of death) (see Dt 28; Rom 5–7; *CCC*, 1502). We all have places in our hearts where we have experienced the disappointment of love, discouragement over a loss of purpose, and the deadening of our deepest unmet desires. These spiritual deaths are at the root of so much of the hopelessness we experience on a day-to-day basis. Left untended, these pockets of despair can result in profound emptiness and futility that can demoralize our entire life. What began as a small disappointment can lead to a lifetime of disconnection, futility, sickness, and even demise.

The ultimate hopelessness is living without God and without hope in this life and then for all of eternity. This is the reality the Church calls hell. Can you even begin to imagine the torment and despair, the complete and utter hopelessness that exists for those who permanently choose to remain divorced from God and thus eternally cut off from any possibility of life, restoration, or hope?

The Bible refers to this permanent state of separation from God as "the second death." This profoundly disturbing reality is described by the apostle John in the book of Revelation: "Blessed and holy is the one who shares in the first resurrection. The second death has no power over these" (Rv 20:6). "But as for cowards, the unfaithful, the depraved, murderers, the unchaste, sorcerers, idol-worshippers, and deceivers of every sort, their lot is the burning pool of fire and sulfur, which is *the second death*" (Rv 21:8, emphasis added).

The second death has no power over those who share in the first resurrection because in Jesus' resurrection from the dead "death is swallowed up in victory" (1 Cor 15:54). His resurrection offers hope to the entire human race, providing the assurance of life beyond the grave. If we are raised to life in Christ, we are assured that we will see him face to face and be reunited with him and our loved ones for all eternity (see 1 Cor 13:12, 1 Thes 4:13–15). This is the hope offered to us in the sacrament the Church refers to as the Anointing of the Sick.

The Anointing of the Sick is intended to bring healing to those who are sick (and by extension their loved ones) and to prepare the dying for eternal life. In this second aspect, it is sometimes referred to as Last Rites and is coupled with the sacraments of Reconciliation and Holy Communion. I can personally attest to the dramatic impact this sacrament can have in our lives and in the lives of our loved ones. I shared in *Be Healed* about my experience when my brother Dave received this sacrament at the point of death.[4] After receiving the anointing, God brought him back from the edge of death and literally raised him up from his deathbed for two weeks. This brief respite from death provided our family an opportunity to experience reconciliation and healing, bringing lasting hope and encouragement for each one of us.

I also experienced the grace of the sacrament with several members of Margie's family and with a close friend of hers. Only my sister-in-law recovered her health after the anointing, but in every instance we were immensely comforted, knowing that God in his mercy forgave the sins of our loved ones to prepare them for the glory of their resurrection in Christ. In faith, we could trust that they would not undergo the torments of hell but were given the firm hope of enjoying the fullness of heaven. There was a deep peace that descended upon us, knowing that we would one day be reunited with them (provided we too remained in a state of grace).

I know many others who have experienced similar consolations with the sacrament. My friends Lance and Nicole were deeply concerned about his father's salvation. They prayed earnestly for him and were finally reassured when he received this sacrament. But lingering doubts after his passing made Nicole question what they witnessed and whether in fact the sacrament accomplished its stated purpose. The confirmation came a few weeks later, when she was praying one day after receiving Jesus in Holy Communion at daily Mass.

The following is Nicole's description of what transpired when her father-in-law received the Anointing of the Sick and the subsequent vision she received from Jesus during her reflection time after receiving the Eucharist:

> My father-in-law's last week of life was one of the holiest weeks I have experienced in my entire life. It was truly a sacred time of being present to love him and pray for him while taking care of him during the last stage of cancer.
>
> In the beginning of his cancer I witnessed my father-in-law expressing his absolute lack of desire to

receive any of the sacraments of the Church or any
need to be reconciled to the Lord. He had been away
from Jesus and the Church for more than forty years.
I recognized it was a time of pressing in to love him
in this place of vulnerability and entrusting him into
the hands of Our Lady. The intensity of our prayers,
sacrifices, and those of our intimate friends—some of
whom are priests and religious [sisters and brothers]—
increased for him. He was being covered in grace. His
internal wrestling with God was quiet yet felt. It was
amazing to see the steady movement of God in two
short months transform my father-in-law's "no" into
a tender, open "yes."

I clearly remember the day Fr. Tom came to anoint
him and bring Jesus to him. He arrived at three o'clock
in the afternoon; the hour of mercy was not lost on me.
I was not sure how he would respond to Fr. Tom yet
I trusted this was the time. He was led to ask simple
questions: "John, may I pray with you? May I anoint
you? Would you like to receive Jesus?" It was clear
Dad understood what he was being asked and was
ready to receive. After that moment you could see Dad
begin to rest as peace poured into his heart. In turn
profound peace filled the air as it became incredibly
palpable throughout the house. He passed away three
days later.

I remember waking up one December morning
about two weeks after my father-in-law's passing
from this life with the weight of deep doubt creating
such sorrow in my heart as I wondered whether any
of the prayerful intercession and sacrifices did anything at all. I was asking myself: Was it all worth it,
and did any of it have an impact upon Dad? I felt bad
for doubting Jesus' mercy when I know I witnessed
it before my eyes, but I could not shake the painful

sorrow that was leading and touching on a feeling within me of despair. I went to Mass that morning carrying this ache and question in my heart. I longed to know the truth, and all I desired was to be at the feet of Jesus. I literally wanted to place my head upon his feet because I longed for him, because I so deeply needed him. I was so aware of this throughout Mass that during the offering itself, it became my offering of myself to the Father, in union with Jesus.

Once I received Jesus in Communion, I knelt down and could feel the tears fill my eyes and begin to run down my cheeks. I placed myself at his feet, and in my heart I saw the image of Jesus kneeling down to meet me eye to eye. I could feel his loving gaze penetrating my heart, his eyes filled with tears acknowledging my ache, my deep sorrow and yearning. I knew in that moment without words that he shared in this with me, that he knew my ache. Then he gently touched my chin to tenderly *raise me up* to my feet with such a radiant joy in his eyes that I was taken aback as I saw my father-in-law standing next to him. I was so overcome by such a flood of life as I felt my father-in-law embrace me in his arms with such profound love and gratitude. It permeated my heart. Gratitude for every prayer and offering of suffering we made for him not only through the years but especially leading up to the hour of his death. That nothing was in vain. It was so intense in that brief moment yet I knew his deep, deep understanding of all of the sacrifices made for him, and in that, I knew he now understood not only my heart and love for him but also my husband's in a new way. He truly was a transformed man! It was so humbling. All I could do was weep because my Lord came to me in such a vulnerable place that only he could satisfy. Jesus knew the details of my heart and

how to lovingly tend to me. I knew in the depths of
my being that every prayer and sacrifice was not only
worth it but that I was willing to do it all over again.

Jesus wanted to meet me there; he was waiting
for me to come, to invite him into my weakness and
encounter his love. I realize there is but a veil on our
side of this mystery yet knowing in the essence of my
being the reality of the Communion of Saints and the
mystical body of Christ is truly alive.

Beautiful, isn't it? This all began with their prayers of intercession
for Lance's father, followed by his father receiving the Anointing of
the Sick. In her vision, Nicole tasted the reality of heaven and directly experienced the eternal hope that comes through the grace of this
sacrament. Notice that she was feeling despair until Jesus raised her
up and showed her the realities of heaven. Let's stop here to reflect
on all this and apply it personally.

Take a Moment

1. Is Jesus' resurrection real and important in your daily life? How
   does this reality help you overcome hopelessness and fear of
   death?

2. Have you had any personal experience with the sacrament of the
   Anointing of the Sick? If so, how did it provide hope and healing
   for you and/or your loved ones?

—⁂—

Death is the final enemy that all of us must face (see 1 Cor 15:26).
If not for the Gospel's promise of life after death, hopelessness and
despair would be our ultimate reality because hopelessness is the inevitable fruit of death and the wound most closely associated with death
itself. But God provides us a firm anchor of hope in the resurrection

of Jesus, reminding us over and over again that he has defeated death. Throughout the ages, he has continued to demonstrate the power of his resurrection life by healing the sick and raising the dead.

The story of Lazarus is arguably the most well-known account in history of someone being brought back to life. Unlike most of the other raised-from-the-dead accounts in scripture, the story of Lazarus's resurrection allows us to experience the virtue of hope in the midst of the sisters' anguish. Anyone who has lost someone close to him through death knows the gut-wrenching pain that comes from losing the one you love as well as the subsequent disorientation that ensues. After seeing my brother Dave get sick and die, I can readily identify with Mary and Martha as they stood by helplessly watching their brother Lazarus get sick and then die (see Jn 11).[5] Jesus, too, loved Lazarus like a brother. I can readily imagine him being deeply distraught upon hearing the news that his close friend had died after a sudden illness.

The narrative in John's gospel begins with Mary and Martha sending word to Jesus urging him to come quickly: "Master, the one you love is ill" (Jn 11:3). They knew with great confidence that Jesus could heal their brother because they watched Jesus respond time after time to the requests of others for healing. Jesus never failed to respond. But for some inexplicable reason, Jesus delayed in answering their plea. When he finally did arrive several days later, Lazarus not only was dead but also had been in the tomb for four days. The sisters appear none too pleased when Jesus finally showed up. I detect a mixture of faith and angst in Martha's first words to Jesus: "Lord, if you had been here, my brother would not have died" (Jn 11:21). Nevertheless, she continued to hold on to hope: "Even now I know that whatever you ask of God, God will give you" (Jn 11:22).

Jesus responded to Martha: "Your brother will rise" (Jn 11:23). He then offered her the promise of eternal hope: "I am the resurrection and the life; whoever believes in me, even if he dies, will live, and everyone who lives and believes in me will never die" (Jn 11:25–26). Martha believed Jesus but didn't quite catch his intention; she thought Jesus was referring only to the resurrection on the last day. Moments later, her sister, Mary, while weeping, repeated almost verbatim what her sister had said: "Lord, if you had been here, my brother would not have died" (Jn 11:32). Apparently moved with great affection and compassion for the sisters' pain, Jesus also began to weep.

I find it interesting that Jesus is weeping, all the while knowing that Lazarus will be raised up in a few minutes. Isn't it comforting to know that Jesus deeply feels our pain with us? He shows us that God is not a distant and disinterested bystander but one who cares tenderly for us in our losses. This in itself brings a profound sense of hope. He who has ultimate power over death still sympathizes with us in our weaknesses and shares in our sufferings (see Heb 4:15). Yet he suffers with hope, knowing that death has no ultimate power when we turn to him.

—◊—

Is there a more dramatic scene in the gospels than this one where Lazarus is brought back to life after four days of decay and stench? Perhaps Jesus' own resurrection appearances compare favorably, but other than that, I am hard-pressed to think of a more compelling miracle in the scriptures. Though I have seen many people healed of various ailments, I have never personally witnessed a miracle of this magnitude, where someone is brought back to life after he has died. Have you? Do you believe it is possible in our day and age?

A quarter of a century ago, I discovered that it is more than possible when I went to visit my brother Bart at the Institute for Ministry in Bradenton, Florida. Most of Bart's classmates were missionaries from foreign countries, and the majority had personally witnessed and participated in this miracle of raising someone from the dead. Yes, you heard me correctly. Bart and I were the exceptions. We felt like kindergartners in a room full of spiritually mature people. As you can imagine, we were utterly amazed as we listened attentively to their stories. Since then we have heard hundreds of other testimonies like that going on throughout the world and hundreds more from the testimonies of saints down through the ages.

Recently, someone gave me a copy of *Raised from the Dead*, a book written by Fr. Albert Hebert. In it, Fr. Hebert chronicles the miracles performed by canonized saints and many others who obeyed Jesus' command to "cure the sick, raise the dead, . . . drive out demons" (Mt 10:8). I had never heard most of these testimonies before. I wonder how many people in our era have.

Did you know that some of the most well-known saints—such as St. Ambrose, St. Patrick, St. Benedict, St. Bernard, St. Catherine of Siena, St. Teresa of Avila, St. Francis Xavier, and many others in every era of the Church—prayed for someone to be raised from the dead and watched the miracle take place before their very eyes? They simply took Jesus at his word and obeyed his commandment to "heal the sick and raise the dead."

Some, like St. Patrick, St. Hyacinth, and St. Anthony of Padua, saw as many as forty, fifty, and one hundred people raised from the dead. Through their prayers in the authority of Jesus Christ, thousands more were healed and delivered from evil. In a few of the accounts, the dead were raised only to be baptized or to receive the sacrament of Reconciliation before being allowed to die again in peace so they wouldn't be subject to the second death. Their family members were given the assurance of their salvation, just like Lance and Nicole were with Lance's dad.

Do those testimonies inspire you and increase your faith and hope? Or do they disturb you and cause you to question and doubt? For me, these stories are both inspiring and disturbing. I am inspired by God's love and the faith of his people. And I am confident these miracles proved to be a tremendous source of grace for many of those who were on the receiving end of the miracles and healings and many others who saw or heard their testimonies. But these testimonies also show me how little I trust in God's goodness and power.

When I examine my own experiences in light of the saints and others who trust God at his word, I see how little faith I have and how much all of us have been influenced by a post-Enlightenment Christianity, which intellectualizes our faith while denying God's presence and powerful intervention in our lives. Unlike Mary and Martha, and these other saints down through the ages, most of us don't *expect* Jesus to heal us or our loved ones. And the great majority of us certainly don't believe he will raise anyone from the dead. Wouldn't most of us be shocked if he did?

Many of the testimonies I have heard in modern times of people being raised from the dead come from Africa, where this post-Enlightenment bias is not as pervasive. I love how Bishop Robert Barron speaks to this issue: "The Church is growing in Africa, not because people are poorly educated, but because the version of Christianity on offer there is robustly supernatural. . . . African Christianity puts a powerful stress on the miraculous, on eternal life, on the active providence of God, on healing grace, and on the divinity of Jesus. If such an emphasis is naive, then every biblical author, every doctor of the Church, and every major theologian until the nineteenth century was naive. The reason a supernaturally oriented Christianity grows is that it is congruent with the purposes of the Holy Spirit."[6]

You may wonder what Bishop Barron means when he speaks of the purposes of the Holy Spirit. The *Catechism* provides a clear and direct answer, which is a summation of the scriptures and Church teaching over the centuries: "The desire and work of the Spirit in the heart of the Church is that we may live from the life of the risen Christ" (*CCC*, 1091). It goes on to say that every sacrament is intended by the Holy Spirit to be an encounter with the risen Christ.

—⁂—

How much does our post-Enlightenment skepticism keep us from seeing more healing and miracles in the sacraments, especially in the Anointing of the Sick, which is given to the Church for this express purpose? Do we really approach the sacrament anticipating that Jesus will "heal the sick, raise the dead, and cast out demons"? Or do we believe that we have to be a missionary or saint for that to happen in our world? I wonder how many of us believe it is possible that Jesus could do those things today but we don't want to get our hopes up only to be disappointed.

What if we approached the Anointing of the Sick (and all the sacraments) with the kind of trust in Jesus that Mary and Martha exhibited? They came in with an unrelenting desire and hope that Jesus would heal their brother and believed Jesus could raise him up. They believed Jesus cared for them and Lazarus and trusted that he would intervene in some way; otherwise they wouldn't have sent for him. They were obviously disappointed and heartbroken when Jesus didn't get there sooner, before their brother died, but they also surrendered themselves to his purposes, for God's greater glory.

God ended up doing much more than they could have imagined. What if we came to the sacrament with a similar posture, placing our hope in Jesus, who is "the resurrection and the life," and approaching him with an unrelenting desire for his intervention? He will always do more than we can imagine and often more than we can visibly see with our human perception.

The Church believes firmly in "the life-giving presence of Christ, the physician of souls and bodies" and trusts that Jesus is always touching us through the sacraments to bring about our healing (see *CCC*, 1504, 1509). The Church also recognizes that not everyone is miraculously healed, and fewer still are raised from the dead, on this side of death. But through it all, the Church believes firmly in the resurrection of the dead (see *CCC*, 1505, 1508).

Miracles happen much more often than we are aware. But not all of God's interventions are visible to the human eye. Healing is regularly occurring without our awareness. This healing, deliverance, and new life taking place in our spirits and souls often reaches the depths of our sin, hopelessness, and despair. This is the first grace of the Anointing of the Sick:

> The first grace of this sacrament is one of strengthening, peace, and courage to overcome the difficulties that go with the condition of serious illness or the

frailty of old age. This grace is a gift of the Holy Spirit, who renews trust and faith in God and strengthens against the temptations of the evil one, the *temptation to discouragement and anguish* in the face of death. This assistance from the Lord by the power of his Spirit is meant to lead the sick person to *healing of the soul,* but *also of the body* if such is God's will. Furthermore, "if he has committed sins, he *will be forgiven.*" (*CCC,* 1520, emphasis added)

These graces are ones Lance's father received when he was anointed with the blessed oil. Was his miracle any less than the forty people St. Patrick brought back from the dead when he prayed for them? It may seem less spectacular to the world, but with the eyes of faith, it is just as much a "raising up" in Christ, from death into life.

Healing and miracles often increase our hope, but they are not the *basis for our hope.* We have another more trustworthy, rock-solid foundation for our hope: the person, Jesus Christ, who describes himself as "the resurrection and the life." He told Martha, anyone who believes in him will never die (see Jn 11:25–26). Holding firm to this hope, we are promised a share in his life. All of us who believe in the Resurrection are already "raised to life." This is our hope. Let's take a moment to reflect more deeply on these matters.

Take a Moment

1. Do you believe that Jesus' command "to cure the sick, raise the dead, . . . cast out demons" is meant for you? Explain.

2. What are your reactions to the stories of the saints who raised the dead? Do these stories inspire faith or doubt in your heart? Explain.

3. What does the Church teach about how the Anointing of the Sick heals wounds of hopelessness? How has the sacrament given you hope?

—ᘏᕆ—

Scripture Meditation

The following passage from John 11 is the account of Jesus raising Lazarus from the dead. I encourage you to reflect on this passage, asking the Holy Spirit for personal revelation. Read it three times, each with a different focus.

Ask the Holy Spirit to guide you as your read and reflect on this passage.

1. Read the passage the first time for overall understanding.

2. As you read slowly again the second time, put yourself in the place of one or both of the sisters and pay attention to what you experience. Then record it in a journal.

3. As you read it the third time, identify with Jesus this time. Pay attention to what you think, feel, and desire, and then record these insights.

Jesus Raises Lazarus from the Dead

"When Jesus arrived, he found that Lazarus had already been in the tomb for four days. Now Bethany was near Jerusalem, only about two miles away. And many of the Jews had come to Martha and Mary to comfort them about their brother. When Martha heard that Jesus was coming, she went to meet him; but Mary sat at home. Martha said to Jesus, 'Lord, if you had been here, my brother would not have died. [But] even now I know that whatever you ask of God, God will give you.' Jesus said to her, 'Your brother will rise.' Martha said to him, 'I know he will rise, in the resurrection on the last day.' Jesus told her, 'I am the resurrection and the life; whoever believes in me, even if he dies, will live, and everyone who lives and believes in me will never die. Do you believe this?' She said to him, 'Yes, Lord. I have come to believe that you are the Messiah, the Son of God, the one who is coming into the world.' When she had said this, she went and called her sister Mary secretly, saying, 'The teacher is here and is asking for you.' As soon as she heard this, she rose quickly and went to him. For Jesus had not yet come into the village, but was still where Martha had met him. So when the Jews who were with her in the house comforting her saw Mary get up quickly and go out, they followed her, presuming that she was going to the tomb to weep there. When Mary came to where Jesus was and saw him, she fell at his feet and said to him, 'Lord, if you had been here, my brother would not have died.' When Jesus saw her weeping and the Jews who had come with her weeping, he became perturbed and deeply troubled, and said, 'Where have you laid him?' They said to him, 'Sir, come and see.' And Jesus wept. So the Jews said, 'See how he loved him.' But some of them said, 'Could not the one who opened the eyes of the blind man have done something so that this man would not have died?' So Jesus, perturbed again, came to the tomb. It was a cave, and a stone lay across it. Jesus said, 'Take away the stone.' Martha, the dead man's sister, said to him, 'Lord, by now there will be a stench; he has been dead for four days.' Jesus said to her, 'Did I not tell you that if you believe you will see the glory of God?' So they took away the stone. And Jesus raised his eyes and said, 'Father, I thank you for hearing me. I know that you always hear me; but because of the crowd here I have said this, that they may believe that you sent me.' And when he had said this, he cried out in a loud voice, 'Lazarus, come out!' The dead man came out, tied hand and foot with burial bands, and his face was wrapped in a cloth. So Jesus said to them, 'Untie him and let him go'" (Jn 11:17–44).

Let Us Pray

Hopelessness is a fruit of spiritual death. All of us have wounds of hopelessness in our lives: areas where we have been cut off from the love we desire, where our dreams have been thwarted, and where we don't see that something good is coming on the horizon. The resurrection of Jesus brings hope into these areas of our hearts. In the following prayer experience, I encourage you to invite the Holy Spirit to transform a specific area of hopelessness in your life. Ask the resurrected Jesus to be present to you now, remembering that "the desire and work of the Holy Spirit . . . is that we may live from the life of the risen Christ" (*CCC*, 1091).

1. Ask the Holy Spirit to reveal an area where you have experienced hopelessness.

2. Then, invite Jesus to show you what he desires for you to know in this area of your life. (Listen with your heart and record what you "hear" from him. It may be revealed through a thought, image, desire, or feeling.)

3. What is Jesus revealing to you in the situation? Test what you receive. If it is from Jesus you will notice the fruits—love, joy, peace, and hope. Go back to the previous experience that felt hopeless, and see if there is more hope.

4. Continue this prayer, over time, until your hopelessness is transformed into an enduring sense of hope in this area of your life.

5. Finish the prayer by thanking Jesus for his resurrection life and for bringing that life inside of you.

CONCLUSION

*His divine power has bestowed on us every-
thing that makes for life and devotion.*

2 Peter 1:3

It might seem like a strange comparison, but *The Lion King* is a re-
freshing representation of the Gospel message and a fitting way to
summarize much of what I have tried to communicate in the preceding
pages. Like many good movies with a redemptive theme,[1] it awakens
in us a longing for our ultimate mission and calls us into our true
identity, after some much-needed healing and transformation.

In the animated movie version, the main character, Simba, is a
young lion and the son of Mufasa, the Lion King. He is the rightful
heir to his father's throne. But after his father's tragic death at the
hands of the evil Scar, Simba loses touch with his identity. Scar lies to
him about who he is, blaming him for his father's death and wounding him deeply (Simba experiences all seven of the deadly wounds).
Destined to follow in his father's footsteps as the Lion King, Simba
instead ends up running away from his most high calling, finding himself in an illusory happy-land singing meaningless songs of self-in-
dulgence: "Hakuna Matata," which means: "Don't worry, be happy."

Simba represents each one of us, who are sons of the Father and
coheirs with the Lion of Judah (see Rom 8:14–17, Rv 2:26). As we
have discussed throughout this book, we are each personally and
uniquely called to embark on this journey of discovering our true
identity as the offspring of the King. But like Simba, we forget who
we are and run away from our calling, spending our precious time
living from a false self, in some illusory "happy-land." Eventually, we
find out that "happy-land" is actually "empty-ville." But, much like
Simba, we don't know our way home. We need a guide in our lives

(the Holy Spirit) to bring us back to our senses and to remind us of our true identity and authentic mission.

In one of the most climactic scenes in the movie, the monkey Rafi-ki, who represents the Holy Spirit, comes to find Simba to bring him back to his homeland. But first he must bring about a transformation of his heart by *reminding* him of his true identity and calling. After a long and winding journey, through much underbrush and past many obstacles, Rafiki leads Simba to a pond where he is encouraged to look at his reflection in "the mirror." As he gazes deeply at himself, Simba sees the reflection of his father, the Lion King. And at that same moment he hears his father's voice from heaven thundering these words: "Remember who you are."

As you might imagine, this is the turning point in Simba's life and the beginning of his reign as king of the land. Rafiki encourages him to let go of the past and look with hope to the future. When he finally returns to his homeland, Simba saves his people from the evil clutches of Scar and his companions. The kingdom is transformed from darkness into light, from the clutches of death into the freedom of life.

The Lion King is a beautiful example of how movies can speak to the hearts of all generations. The priests attending our recent Holy Desire conference loved the movie as much as my grandchildren, who have watched the movie several times. After finding out that we borrowed their movie to show the priests, my grandsons Jack and Luke (ages nine and seven at the time) asked me if the priests liked the movie and "got it" (i.e., understood the spiritual symbolism). Then they began to explain to me who each of the characters represented and what the movie meant for each of us.

They told me that Mufasa represented the Father and Jesus, and Simba represented Jesus and each of us. They laughed as they thought about the monkey Rafiki being like the Holy Spirit; and they readily identified the evil Scar as the representation of Satan, the father of lies. They told me the hyenas were like demons, and other characters represented angels that are sent to guard us. They even understood that Simba had to remember who he was before he could fulfill his role as Lion King. I sat there amazed listening to them, and then added a few insights they hadn't considered.

I told them the scene where Simba saw his reflection in the pond was like Jesus' Baptism, where the Father spoke from heaven: "This is my beloved Son in whom I am well pleased." (Providentially, this was the gospel that day at church and they discussed it in children's church.) When I asked them if they understood that these words are meant for them, too, they asked me to explain. I told them that all the sacraments in our lives are like Jesus' Baptism. "Through the priest, the Father speaks his blessing over our lives, just as he did for Jesus. When we pray and read the scriptures we get to hear the Father speak to our hearts. That means, Jack and Luke, you are the Father's beloved, like Jesus, and like Simba. You are lion kings! Jesus lives in you and you are called to do great things with your life. Remember who you are!"

While I could tell they enjoyed hearing me remind them of these realities, they already knew most of what I told them because it is written in their hearts. Their parents, siblings, aunts, uncles, grandparents, and teachers have been telling them these kinds of things since they were born. They are still young, and though they have been wounded already by the lies of the enemy, they still have firm hope that they will do something great with their lives. They haven't lost sight of their true identity or lost trust in the Father's goodness. I am deeply grateful that our children have passed on to our grandchildren these greatest of all gifts.

Passing our faith down through the generations is vitally important. When I think about this in my life, I realize how I, too, received blessings of my identity and calling from my grandparents and parents throughout my life. My grandmother Margaret was the first person in my life to tell me I was going to be a writer (I was around Luke and

Jack's age). When I gave her a signed autographed copy of my first book some fifty years later, I reminded her of her encouragement. At ninety-seven, she is still going strong and still affirming my identity and calling. My grandfather, too, was a great encourager before he died at the ripe old age of ninety-three.

My parents are both alive, and both of them are great encouragers in my life. I am grateful to God for the healing in our family that allows even our brokenness to reveal his glory. In the past several years, both my mom and dad have come to our conferences and given brief testimonies about God's goodness and redemption. And to this day they never quit praying for us or encouraging us. Just a few minutes ago, as I was praying how to end this book, I received a phone call from my mom, interrupting me in the middle of writing. She said, "I was just praying and reflecting on these words from my devotional. I felt like I needed to call you immediately because, as I read this reflection, it seemed like it might fit for your book." I trusted it must have been the Holy Spirit speaking through her because, at that point, my mom didn't know what I was writing.

Here is what she shared with me in her devotional from Fr. Thomas Keating. I will let you be the judge whether this provides a good mirror for you to remember who you are in Christ:

> God's will for us is to manifest God's goodness and infinite tenderness in our lives right now. Christian tradition is not merely a handing on of various doctrines and rituals. It is the handing on of "the experience of the living Christ," revealed in the scripture, preserved in the sacraments, and received in every act of prayer, and present in a special way in the major events of our lives. If we are open and available to this presence, our lives will be transformed. The spiritual journey is a struggle to be ever more available to God and to let go of the obstacles to that transforming process. The gospel is not merely an invitation to be a better

person. It is an invitation to become divine. It invites
us to share the interior life of the Trinity.[2]

As my mom read those words to me over the phone, I couldn't believe how much they expressed what I wanted to convey to conclude this book. As Fr. Keating noted, Christianity is a handing on of the "experience of the living Christ." His abiding presence is conveyed through the sacraments, most fully in Holy Communion. We come to know him more intimately through the scriptures and in every act of authentic prayer. Our journey is a struggle, with many obstacles (sin and deadly wounds) that must be healed. But if we will submit ourselves and make ourselves available, we will take on Christ's life and identity as our own, and take our part in his mission to bring all of humanity back into that communion with the Trinity.

The question we each have to ask ourselves is this: Am I willing to allow the Father to bless me in this way and to allow him to uproot the curses in my life so that I can more fully reflect his glory?

As we end here, let's take a final moment to reflect on what we have discussed throughout the book and in this conclusion. Then I invite you to spend time meditating on this passage from 2 Peter 1. Finally, the prayer experience at the end is a summation of the major points we addressed throughout the book. Pray it often to remind yourself of who you are in Christ. Because, as St. John Paul II exhorted all of us, "You are not the sum of your weaknesses or failures. You are the sum of the Father's love for you and your real capacity to become the image of his Son."[3]

Take a Moment

1. Go through the book and write down each of the title chapters. Name the deadly wounds and life-giving sacraments discussed in those chapters. What do these titles tell you about HIM, including your healing, identity, and mission in Christ?

2. Which "Take a Moment" reflection questions, scripture medita-
   tions, and prayer activities had the biggest impact on the way you
   understand God, yourself, and your mission?

3. How has your understanding of the sacraments changed? How
   has this impacted your relationship with Jesus? Be specific.

—ɯ—

Scripture Meditation

The following scripture from 2 Peter 1 is the one referred to earlier in
the devotional from Fr. Keating. This provides an overall context for
the passage and an opportunity for you to enter more deeply into these
insights as you reflect on your identity in Christ. Notice the blessing!
Read through the passage three times, making note and recording
what the Holy Spirit is revealing to you each time.

Partakers of the Divine Nature

"May grace and peace be yours in abundance through knowledge
of God and of Jesus our Lord. His divine power has bestowed on us
everything that makes for life and devotion, through the knowledge of
him who called us by his own glory and power. Through these, he has
bestowed on us the precious and very great promises, so that through
them you may come to share in the divine nature, after escaping the
corruption that is in the world because of evil desire. . . . Therefore,
brothers, be all the more eager to make your call and election firm,
for, in doing so you will never stumble. For, in this way, entry into
the eternal kingdom of our Lord and savior Jesus Christ will be richly
provided for you" (2 Pt 1:2–4, 10–11).

Let Us Pray

The following prayer is a compilation of all that we have discussed. It involves you renouncing the false identity associated with each of the deadly wounds and a proclamation of your true identity, based in the sacraments and affirmed in scripture. As you renounce and proclaim in prayer, allow these realities to penetrate your mind and heart. Invite the Father, Jesus, and the Holy Spirit to fill you, while also blocking the father of lies and his demons from lying to you. I encourage you to type out this prayer and carry it with you so that you can pray with it frequently. Notice how the prayer is organized around the seven deadly wounds, the healing sacraments, and the new identities in Christ that reflect our oneness with him (see the table on page 30).

The Father's Love Heals Rejection
In the name of Jesus Christ, I renounce the lie that I am unloved and unlovable.

In Jesus' name, I announce the truth that by virtue of my Baptism, I am a beloved son or daughter of the Father. I announce the truth that I am loved and valued, wanted and desired, and that I am precious in the Father's eyes.

Jesus' Abiding Presence Heals Abandonment
In the name of Jesus Christ, I renounce the lie that I am alone, unprotected, and that God has abandoned me.

In Jesus' name, I announce the truth that Jesus lives and dwells in me by virtue of my receiving him in Holy Communion. I am connected, understood, and cared for. Jesus and the Communion of Saints are always with me.

The Holy Spirit's Power Heals Powerlessness
In the name of Jesus Christ, I renounce the lie that I am powerless, weak, not capable, stuck, trapped,

or helpless. I renounce the lie that I am a victim and can't change.

In Jesus' name, I announce the truth that I have been anointed in Confirmation with the power of the Holy Spirit to share in Christ's mission, therefore, "I have the strength for everything through him who empowers me" (Phil 4:13).

Jesus' Submission to the Father's Authority Heals Confusion

In the name of Jesus Christ, I renounce the lie that everything is chaotic and confusing and that it is up to me to figure things out on my own.

In Jesus' name, I announce the truth that Jesus has shown me the path to the Father. I reclaim his divine order through the Church, through the sacrament of Holy Orders, and trust this authority to reveal the truth and guide my path.

Jesus' Faithful Love Heals Fear

In the name of Jesus Christ, I renounce the lie that if I trust I will be hurt, disappointed, or die. I renounce all fear, anxiety, mistrust, and distrust.

In Jesus' name, I announce the truth that in Christ perfect love casts out all fear. I announce the truth that I am secure in Jesus' faithful love, which is signified in the sacrament of Matrimony.

Jesus' Purity Heals Shame

In the name of Jesus Christ, I renounce the lie that I am bad, dirty, ugly, stupid, worthless, perverted, and (fill in any area of struggle).

In Jesus' name, I announce the truth that Jesus died for my sins and wounds and that I am forgiven, washed, cleansed, justified, and accepted (see 1 Cor 6). I announce the truth that through the sacrament of

Reconciliation, Jesus washes me clean and forgives my sin; therefore, in Jesus I am pure and undefiled.

Jesus' Resurrection Life Heals Hopelessness
In the name of Jesus Christ, I renounce the lie that nothing ever changes and I will never have what I want. I renounce the lie that my life is meaningless and that I have nothing to live for.

In Jesus' name, I announce the truth, revealed in the Anointing of the Sick, that my hope is steadfast in Christ, and that I have been raised to life in him. My final hope is in the resurrection from the dead and eternal life with the Trinity and the Communion of Saints (see Jn 21:5).

I pray all of this in the powerful name of the Father, the Son, and the Holy Spirit. Amen.

ACKNOWLEDGMENTS

Every book is inspired by a lifetime of relationships and influences that shape who we are as persons. I am grateful to God for each of you in my life who have helped shape me.

Margie, thank you for your support and love over all these years. You have the same kind and generous heart as the day I met you. I am grateful for our sacrament that has sustained us so that we could enjoy our beautiful family together all these years. Carrie and Kristen, you have been a source of great joy since the time you were born. I rejoice in all we have shared together, including all the sacraments that we've shared. I am grateful that these are as important to both of you and your families. Duane and Stephen, you are answers to our lifelong prayers for our daughters. Thank you both for being good men who love God and desire to live the sacraments faithfully. Anna, Drew, Ryan, Jack, Luke, Lily, Elle, and Will, how can grandparents even describe the love we have for you, our grandchildren? You are each so uniquely gifted and beautiful. My heart is filled with love as I think of each of you. I am deeply grateful to your parents and to you, that you have Jesus and his sacraments at the center of your lives.

Mom and Dad, thank you for love and affirmation and for guiding us to find our identity and mission in Christ. Thank you also for introducing us to Christ's resurrection life in the sacraments. Dave, Kathy, Lauren, Wayne, Bart, Margaret, Rich, Missy and Paul, and to your spouses and children, you all have enriched my life in many ways. Thank you for who you are and for your love for God and each other. To all my in-laws, grandparents, aunts, uncles, cousins, and friends through the years, you have each been an integral part of my life. Thank you for your love. I love each one of you.

To all our staff, board, volunteers, intercessors, ministry partners, and supporters at John Paul II Healing Center: I love and appreciate each of you. Thank each of you for living the depth of your sacraments with genuine love for Jesus. I am grateful for your encouragement and for walking this road together, in bringing transformation in the heart of the Church.

For all of you who agreed to let me share your stories in this book, thank you. I pray that your humble witness will not only glorify God but also give hope to many others. You have been a great witness to the healing power of the sacraments.

Many people have had a direct influence on the development of this book, none more than my editor at Ave Maria Press, Kristi Mc-Donald. Kristi, as I have said to you personally, you are a gifted editor and have made this book much better than it would be without you. My gratitude also goes to all the good people at Ave Maria Press who took part in the development and promotion of this book.

I also want to thank each of you who took the time to read and give input on earlier drafts of this book along the way: Carrie, Kristen, Stephen, Anna, Ken, Bart, Mom, Kim, Judy, Fr. Michael, Fr. Tom, Sr. Caritas, Sr. Mary Peter, Ray, Jim, Lois, Lance, Nicole, John, Krista, Terese, Kaitlin, Ellie, and Corinne. And likewise to those who graciously agreed to review and offer your endorsement for this book: Audrey, Christopher, Sr. Miriam, Paul, Mary, and Fr. Dave. I appreciate your encouragement and your living witness to the transforming power of the sacraments. You each embody a unique aspect of Jesus' identity and mission, and have dedicated yourselves to being conduits of his healing presence.

Finally, as I mentioned in the beginning this book is dedicated to St. John Paul II, whose witness and work have formed and shaped me and millions of others around the world. His insights are reflected throughout this book. Thank you, John Paul, for your inspirational reflections on the nature of redeemed man and your holy example of life. You embodied this reality of the healing power of the sacraments and allowed yourself to be transformed by the Holy Spirit working through you, right up until your final breath—and beyond.

Glory be to the Father, the Son, and the Holy Spirit. Amen!

NOTES

Introduction

1. This acronym (HIM) is an adaptation of one taught in the Institute for Priestly Formation. It uses the acronym RIM—Relationships, Identity, Mission. I am grateful for Fr. Chris Celantanno for the inspiration when he presented RIM at a parish mission at Good Shepherd Catholic Church (in Tallahassee, Florida) in February 2016.

2. John Paul II, *Dominum et Vivificantem* (*On the Holy Spirit*), 67.

3. Second Vatican Council, *Gaudium et Spes* (On the Church in the Modern World), 22.

4. Ibid., 24.

1. Unveiled Faces

1. Pope Francis, *Misericordiae Vultus* (*The Face of Mercy*), Bull of Indiction of the Extraordinary Year of Mercy, April 11, 2015.

2. Jacques Philippe, *Interior Freedom* (New York: Scepter Publisher, 2007), 122.

3. Pope Francis, *Rigidity Is a Sign of a Weak Heart*, December 15, 2014, http://en.radiovaticana.va.

4. Philippe, *Interior Freedom*, 124.

5. Francis, Homily (with announcement of year of mercy), March 3, 2015 http://en.radiovaticana.va/news/pope-francis/homilies.

6. This is an adaptation of a prayer from Dr. Karl Lehman. You can find more on judgments and other prayers on his website: kclehman.com.

2. God's Powerful Blessings

1. Neal Lozano, *Unbound* (Grand Rapids, MI: Chosen Book, 2010), 108.

2. Ibid., 109.

3. Masaru Emoto, *The Hidden Messages in Water* (New York: Atria Books, 2004).

4. John Eldredge, *Waking the Dead* (Nashville, TN: Thomas Nelson Publishers, 2003), 152–155.

5. John Paul II, *Dominum et Vivificantem* (*On the Holy Spirit*), 33.

6. I propose throughout this book that Adam and Eve experienced the effects of all seven of these deadly wounds. Jesus took these curses upon himself on the

cross and shared in our suffering with all seven deadly wounds. See chapters 7 and 8 of *Be Healed* for more on this.

7. As I mentioned in *Be Healed*, a list of eight wounds was presented by Dr. Ed Smith in the appendix of his book *Beyond Tolerable Recovery*. This list of wounds resonated with my own experience in accompanying people over many years. I modified his list to seven deadly wounds to parallel the seven deadly sins and seven sacraments of the Church. I am not suggesting that this is the only way to categorize our wounds or the lies associated with them. But I do find it helpful to speak of our wounds in an organized and concise way like this.

8. As we discuss in our Healing the Whole Person conferences, wounds are the fertile ground from which sins are conceived, but they are also the result of sins. The second is more obvious. If someone sins against me, I may likely experience fear, powerlessness, rejection, and so on. But it is not as obvious that my anger or lust may be fueled by these same wounds. Remember St. John Paul II's observation: the root of sin is in the lie, which is a denial of the Father's goodness.

9. Dave Pivonka, T.O.R., *Breath of God: Living a Life Led by the Holy Spirit* (Notre Dame, IN: Ave Maria Press, 2015), 114.

3. The Father's Beloved

1. Esther Katz, "Sanger, Margaret" (American National Biography Online, Feb. 2000), http://www.anb.org/articles/15/15-00598.html; Biography.com Editors, "Margaret Sanger Biography" (A&E Television Networks, July 8, 2014), http://www.biography.com/people/margaret-sanger-9471186; Biography of Margaret Sanger, American National Biography online, http://www.anb.org/articles/15/15-00598.html.

2. "Margaret Sanger" (PBS Online, 2001), http://www.pbs.org/wgbh/amex/pill/peopleevents/p_sanger.html.

3. Margaret Sanger, "The Eugenic Value of Birth Control Propaganda," *Birth Control Review*, October 1921, 5; "Margaret Sanger, Racist Eugenicist Extraordinaire" (*Washington Times*, May 5, 2014), http://www.washingtontimes.com/news/2014/may/5/grossu-margaret-sanger-eugenicist/.

4. Margaret Sanger, "The Woman Rebel: No God's, No Masters" (March 1914, 1, 8, 16); Diane Drew, "Margaret Sanger, In Her Own Words," www.Dianedrew.com/sanger/htm; *The Autobiography of Margaret Sanger* (Mineola, NY: Dover Publications Inc., 1971).

5. Kimberly Hahn, *Life-Giving Love* (Ann Arbor, MI: Servant Publications, 2001), 54.

6. Mother Teresa of Calcutta Center, www.motherteresa.org.

7. Raniero Cantalamessa, *Sober Intoxication of the Spirit* (Cincinnati, OH: Servant Books, 2005), 42.

8. To learn what the Bible and the Church teach about Baptism, see Jn 3:5; Acts 2:38; 2 Cor 5:17; Rom 6:3–4; Tt 3:5; *CCC*, 1213, 1234–1245, and 1262–1274.

9. The *Catechism of the Catholic Church*, 1250, states, "Born with a fallen human nature and tainted by original sin, children also have need of the new birth in baptism to be freed from the power of darkness and brought into the realm of the freedom of the children of God, to which all men are called. The sheer gratuitousness of the grace of salvation is particularly manifest in infant baptism. The Church and the parents would deny a child the priceless grace of becoming a child of God were they not to confer baptism shortly after birth."

10. Ignatius of Loyola, *The Spiritual Exercises of St. Ignatius*, trans. Anthony Mottola (New York: Image Books, 1964), 129–134; William Watson, S.J., *Forty Weeks: An Ignatian Path to Christ with Sacred Story Prayer* (Seattle: Sacred Story Press, 2013), 216, 217.

11. Henri Nouwen, *Life of the Beloved* (New York: The Crossroad Publishing Co., 1992), 33.

4. Abiding Presence

1. John Paul II, *Man and Woman He Created Them: A Theology of the Body*, trans. Michael Waldstein (Boston, MA: Pauline Books and Media, 2006), 9:2.

2. John Paul II, World Youth Day 2000 (Rome) Closing Mass Homily, August 20, 2000.

3. John Paul II, World Youth Day 2000 (Rome) Closing Mass Homily, August 20, 2000.

4. Francis, Homily at Sunday Mass, December 1, 2013, reported by Kerri Lenartowick, *Catholic News Agency*, www.catholicnewsagency.com/news/christian-life-is-a-path-of-encountering-jesus-preaches-pope.

5. See chapter 9 of *Be Healed*, where I share stories of healing through the Eucharist.

6. Thomas Keating, *The Daily Reader for Contemplative Living* (New York: Continuum International Publishing Group, 2009), 46.

7. This is a modified version of the contemplative prayer process attributed to Dr. Karl Lehman, a Christian psychiatrist. See ImmanuelApproach.com.

5. Anointed with Power

1. See John and Staci Eldridge, *Captivating* (Nashville, TN: Thomas Nelson Publisher, 2005), 46–59, for a discussion on these dynamics.

2. The Church calls this weakness concupiscence, following 1 John 2:16—lust of the flesh, lust of the eyes, and the pride of life.

3. All of this is described in more detail in chapter 1 of *Be Healed*.

4. John Eldridge, in his book *Wild at Heart* (Nashville, TN: Thomas Nelson Publisher, 2001), says that every young boy has this question: "Do I have what it takes?" When a boy has a father wound, this quest becomes even more heightened.

5. This experience is described in detail in chapter 1 of *Be Healed*.

6. Mary Healy, *Healing* (Huntingdon, IN: Our Sunday Visitor Inc., 2015), 28.

7. Raniero Cantalamessa, *Come Creator Spirit* (Collegeville, MN: Liturgical Press, 2003), 153.

8. George T. Montague, S.M., *Holy Spirit, Make Your Home in Me* (Ijamsville, MD: The Word Among Us Press, 2008), 154.

6. The Father's Authority

1. For those interested in more of the back story to this, see chapter 2: The Good Teacher, in my book *Be Healed.*

2. John Paul II, *Crossing the Threshold of Hope* (New York: Alfred A. Knopf, 1994), 228; emphasis added.

3. Ignatius of Antioch, in William Jurgens, *The Faith of the Early Fathers,* vol. 1 (Collegeville, MN: Liturgical Press), 17–25.

4. For more on this, see "Beloved Sons to Faithful Fathers" in the CD set for priests, seminarians, and deacons at www.jpiihealingcenter.org. It is the first talk in a three-part series titled *Sharing in Jesus' Humanity and Priesthood.*

5. This is a pseudonym to protect the priest's confidentiality.

6. United States Conference of Catholic Bishops, *Program for Priestly Formation*, sec. 23.

7. Gregory Nazianzus, quoted in the *Catechism of the Catholic Church*, 1589.

7. God's Faithful Love

1. John Paul II, *Familiaris Consortio* (*The Family in the Modern World*), secs. 11, 14, 17, 18.

2. James Friesen, James Wilder, et al., *The Life Model* (Pasadena, CA: Shepherds House Inc., 2004), 28, 31.

3. Ibid.

4. For more on inner vows, see chapter 7: Anatomy of a Wound, in *Be Healed.*

5. I tell this story in chapters 1 and 9 of *Be Healed.*

6. See *Unveiled: Discovering the Great Mystery in Your Marriage*, page 14 (workbook and CDs available at www.jpiihealingcenter.org).

8. Pure and Undefiled

1. Merriam-Webster.com/dictionary/shame, 1, 2.

2. John Paul II, *Man and Woman*, 16:3.

3. Ibid., 12:4.

4. Cantalamessa, *Come Creator Spirit*, 116.

5. Ibid.

6. John Paul II, *Reconciliation and Penance*, quoted in the *Catechism of the Catholic Church*, 1469.

7. I gave Hank a copy of the book *The Peacemaker* by Ken Sande (Grand Rapids, MI: Baker Books, 1991). Chapter 6 describes the parts of a good confession:

(1) directly facing the one hurt, (2) taking full responsibility, (3) repenting of both wrong attitudes and behaviors, (4) addressing the pain caused to the injured, (5) making a firm commitment to change, (6) accepting the consequences for our wrongs and making restitution where possible, and (7) then humbly asking for forgiveness.

8. Francis, *Misericordiae Vultus* (*Bull of Indiction of the Extraordinary Jubilee Year of Mercy*), 1, 17.

9. Raised to Life

1. Words of Roman Rite of the Anointing of the Sick contained in the *Catechism of the Catholic Church*, 1513; emphasis added.

2. Is this the origins of the primordial wound of hopelessness? St. Thomas Aquinas asserts that despair (hopelessness) is a result of being cut off from a good that we desire, or not being able to avoid an evil that we don't want. See Fr. Chad Rippenger summarizing the teaching of St. Thomas Aquinas in *Introduction to the Science of Mental Health* (Denton, NE: Sensus Traditius Press, 2007), 151.

3. John Paul II, *Man and Woman*, 4:1.

4. See *Be Healed*, 155–156.

5. The story of Dave's dying process is recounted in chapter 8 of *Be Healed*.

6. Robert Barron, "What Makes the Church Grow?" December 9, 2015, wordonfire.org/resources/articles/5007.

Conclusion

1. In good movies, we come to discover the person we desire to be; in doing so we become more aware of our true identity and calling. I am grateful to John Eldredge for this insight. In many of his writings and conferences, he shares how most good movies have a Christ figure (a savior), those needing to be saved, and a theme of redemption. I draw out this idea in our Holy Desire conferences, work-books, and CDs at the John Paul II Healing Center.

2. Thomas Keating, *The Daily Reader for Contemplative Living* (New York: Continuum International Publishing Group, 2009), 41.

3. John Paul II, Closing Homily at World Youth Day Toronto, July 28, 2002.

Bob Schuchts is the bestselling author of *Be Healed* and founder of the John Paul II Healing Center in Tallahassee, Florida. In December 2014 he retired as a marriage and family therapist after thirty-five years of practice. After receiving his doctorate in family relations from Florida State University in 1981, Schuchts began teaching and counseling. While in private practice, Schuchts also taught graduate and undergraduate courses at Florida State and Tallahassee Community College. Schuchts later served on faculty at the Theology of the Body Institute and at the Center for Biblical Studies, where he taught courses on healing, sexuality, and marriage. He also volunteered in parish ministry for more than thirty years.

Schuchts and his wife, Margie, have two daughters and eight grandchildren. They live in Tallahassee.

AVE

AVE MARIA PRESS

Founded in 1865, Ave Maria Press,
a ministry of the Congregation of
Holy Cross, is a Catholic publishing
company that serves the spiritual and
formative needs of the Church and its
schools, institutions, and ministers;
Christian individuals and families; and
others seeking spiritual nourishment.

For a complete listing of titles from

Ave Maria Press

Sorin Books

Forest of Peace

Christian Classics

visit www.avemariapress.com

AVE MARIA PRESS
Notre Dame, IN

A Ministry of the United States Province of Holy Cross